Teenage Drinking

TEENAGE

THE #1 DRUG THREAT

Robert North and

DRINKING

TO YOUNG PEOPLE TODAY

Richard Orange, Jr.

COLLIER BOOKS
Macmillan Publishing Company
New York

COLLIER MACMILLAN PUBLISHERS
London

TO THE WOMEN IN OUR LIVES:
Mrs. Ola J. Diggs and Mrs. Mary Johnson—
our grandmothers
Mrs. Edith Diggs North and Mrs. Alice M. Orange—
our mothers
Mrs. Pamela Palanque North and
Mrs. Trudy Robinson Orange—our wives
Taur Orange and Barbara North—our sisters
and Blaine Sharon Edith North (8/16/79)
and Courtney Denise Orange (2/15/79)—
our daughters
It begins with you!

Macmillan Publishing Company
866 Third Avenue, New York, N.Y. 10022
Collier Macmillan Canada, Inc.

Library of Congress Cataloging in Publication Data

North, Robert.
Teenage drinking.

1. Alcohol and youth—United
States. 2. Alcoholism—United States—
Prevention. I. Orange, Richard, joint
author. II. Title.
HV5135.N67   362.7′8′2920973   79-24237
ISBN 0-02-053120-6 pbk.

First Collier Books Edition 1980

10 9 8 7 6 5 4

Printed in the United States of America

Macmillan books are available at special discounts
for bulk purchases for sales promotions, premiums,
fund-raising, or educational use. For details, contact:

Special Sales Director
Macmillan Publishing Company
866 Third Avenue
New York, N.Y. 10022

Contents

Foreword

TO RECOGNIZE THE INCREASING PROBLEM of alcohol abuse among our children and youth is to do more than decry the trend toward the early consumption of alcohol and problem drinking. There is a need to understand this troubling situation, to seek solutions, and to develop preventive approaches. This book is a significant effort in this direction.

The problems of alcohol abuse, alcoholism, and the combined use of alcohol and other drugs among preteenagers and teenagers are growing to alarming proportions throughout the country. There are many contributory factors: peer pressure, parental and familial behavior patterns, sociocultural mores, and the environmental context; all contribute to a complex interplay with individual personality. Certainly, the contribution of a media-conscious nation, in which advertising influences ways of coping, is important, as is the easy availability of alcohol in a society where profits seem to hold a higher priority than health.

As this book indicates, some successful efforts have been made to intervene at critical points. These programs recognize that children of alcoholics are at greater risk of becoming alcoholic. They recognize the fact that adolescence is a time of choice in many areas; it presents an opportunity for the constructive use of peer support and understanding. Those services which are most effective build programmatically upon the interrelationship among the individual, the group, and the community. They take into account the importance of ethnic, social, and cultural factors.

By looking at the problem and at the potential for prevention, treatment, and rehabilitation, the authors have contributed to heightening our awareness of both a significant problem and a possible solution. Since we are talking of our children and youth, and thus, of our own future, this attention is not only timely—it is essential.

—JUNE JACKSON CHRISTMAS, M.D.
Commissioner, Department of Mental Health, Retardation and Alcoholism Services, City of New York

Acknowledgments

WE WISH TO THANK OUR EDITOR, Toni Lopopolo, for her ideas and for her abundance of patience and good judgment. Thank you, Gary Wohl, for your support, help, and patience. We wish to recognize and thank Boys Harbor for its assistance, patience, and the opportunity to work with adolescents.

We would also like to thank: Michael Fultz, Taur Orange, Gregory Armstrong, Gordon Christmas, Glenn Ligon, Josephine Cherry, Sherry Gentile, Clarence Wilkins, Matthew Phillips, Barbara Berry, Dr. Jean Thomas Griffin, and all the staff and students of the Boys Harbor Teenage Alcohol Abuse Prevention Program.

Special thanks to Maxine Womble of the Bureau of Alcoholism, New York City, and Heddy Bubbard of NIAAA, who enabled us to learn about the subject.

Finally, thanks to NTL, Karen, Vangie, John, and friends and colleagues of the Graduate Student Professional Development Program at Bethel, Maine.

Introduction

IN RESEARCHING THIS BOOK, we were constantly amazed at
the amount of conflicting information regarding teenage
drinking and alcoholism. A serious and growing problem
appears to be evident, and yet many experts disagree
about both the severity of the problem and the approaches
to its solutions.

Much has been written about alcoholism over the past
twenty years, but a large part of this literature has been of
a scientific or technical nature. What is known about teenage drinking and alcoholism is unfortunately minimal
and for the most part directed to the professionals in the
field.

This book was written primarily for teenagers as a potential tool for learning more about teenage drinking. We
have attempted in this text to integrate information with
ideas, to separate myth from fact, and to combine humor
with the seriousness this subject requires.

This is not the definitive text on teenage drinking. We don't presume to know all the answers. Our experience, however, in a model prevention and education program, has provided us with some rich insight and ideas concerning teenage drinking and alcoholism.

For parents, teachers, and youth workers, we have provided appendixes that offer additional suggestions for their initial intervention in the area of teenage alcoholism, sample programs and questionnaires that we use in our work, and a list of resources from which to obtain assistance and/or literature. We hope these concerned people will find this material helpful in their efforts to educate youth about the dangers of alcohol abuse and to prevent and heal the serious repercussions associated with it. For teenage alcoholism is, after all, everyone's problem.

—DR. ROBERT NORTH, Project Director
RICHARD ORANGE, Jr., Training Director
The Harbor for Young Men and Women
of Boys Harbor, Inc.
New York City, 1979

TEENAGE DRINKING

1 Alcohol and Youth— Everyone's Problem

AMERICA IS LARGELY A DRINKING SOCIETY. Drinking alcohol of various types is acceptable social behavior that affects and permeates virtually every aspect of our culture. From the traditional wedding toast to the ritualistic pouring of champagne at sporting events such as the World Series and the Super Bowl games, we celebrate with liquor. Celebrities like Alice Cooper and Billy Carter have become famous because of their battles with alcohol, and women swoon over, and men hope to emulate, the "macho" of James Coburn as he sells a "lite beer." Alcohol is used by choice for every conceivable social function at some time or another, by the majority of people in this country. Alcohol, however, is still a drug that can be potentially dangerous. Truly, it is the drug of festivals and funerals.

There are approximately 10 million alcoholics in the

1

United States; most certainly, some of these are adolescents. Teenagers who drink excessively are short and tall, black and white, Christian and Jewish, male and female. Some do well in school, others not so well. Some teenagers who drink listen to the Rolling Stones, others listen to the Commodores, and some don't listen to any music at all. In short, teenagers who abuse alcohol are much like yourself, so don't feel it could never happen to you.

Alcohol abuse and alcoholism are serious problems for persons of any age, but for teenagers there are special fears to confront. For some people, particularly adults, the evident rise of teenage drinking is symptomatic of a decline in the traditional values and attitudes of our society. For others, it may confirm opinions—not shared by the authors—that teenagers are irresponsible and cannot make decisions for themselves. There are opinions and counter-opinions, often conflicting and confusing, as to who exactly is drinking and how much. Teenage drinking is a special concern for everyone, and the problem of teenage alcoholism affects everybody, irrespective of race, religion, or social and economic background.

In our experience, two of the greatest lessons that teenagers learn in alcohol-abuse programs for youth are (1) that alcohol is indeed a drug that when used inappropriately can cause illness and can even kill; and (2) that alcoholism is a disease and ranks among the major national health problems, along with cancer and heart disease. In fact, the Department of Health, Education and Welfare considers alcoholism to be this country's most neglected disease.

Alcoholism is a complex, progressive disease that can be treated. Alcoholics are sick, just as people who suffer from heart disease or cancer are sick. If alcoholics are not treated, then permanent damage, physical incapacity, or death can result.

Unfortunately, many of us do not take the drinking of

alcohol seriously. Frequently when we ask teenagers whether or not they drink, they reply with responses that may sound familiar to some of you:

—No, I don't drink. I just have some beer on the weekends.

—No, I don't drink liquor. I only drink wine.

—I'm not a drinker; I just like fruity drinks like sloe gin fizzes and piña coladas.

—Hey, I don't mess with the booze, but I love me some wine.

There are in fact parents who, when finally confronted with the reality that their son or daughter does have a drinking problem, respond by saying: "Well, I don't mind too much if they're drinking; at least they're not using drugs."

Of course, alcohol *is* a drug, and it is our hope that we can show you just how dangerous a drug it can be if used irresponsibly.

Who Is Really Drinking?

During the past five years or so, smoke signals have gone up alerting us to the alarming increase in teenage drinking. Depending on whom you talk to or on what report you read, you almost expect to see teenagers falling down in the streets all over the country. Such is not really the case. Certainly teenagers abusing alcohol is a serious problem. However, considering its seriousness, the number of conflicting definitions regarding the problem is astounding.

For example, alcohol consumption among adolescents is not perceived in the same manner as it is for adults. To be drunk four or more times in a year is generally the standard by which an adolescent is defined as a problem drinker. This, however, is an appreciably lower standard than the one used for adults.

Teenage drinking, additionally, has "negative consequences." If, for example, a group of teenagers are caught drinking beer at a basketball game or a school dance, chances are the severity of the problem will be magnified because teenage drinking is illegal and disapproved of by adults.

In many states, the legal age for buying alcohol is 18. The drinking of alcohol by teenagers, even if it is only an experiment, is often confused with abuse because of its illegality. There are some counselors and researchers in the field of alcoholism who feel that any experimentation at all by teenagers constitutes abuse. Frequently the definitions are ambiguous and almost always dictated by adults.

The hazy concept of adolescence also adds to the problem. In today's society, many 17- and 18-year-olds are, for all practical purposes, adults. Some 18-year-old men and women have jobs and families, and therefore it would be silly to lump them with 13- or 14-year-olds. In many respects the whole idea of "the Teenager" may have gone out with Frankie Avalon and Beach Blanket Bingo movies. The teenagers of yesterday are the young adults of today, and adults would be wise to reassess their definitions.

It is generally believed that teenage drinking is widespread and has increased dramatically in recent years. What gives this theory some validity is that:

1. There are significantly more teenagers around to drink. There were approximately 11 million teenagers (between 15 and 19 years of age) in 1960. Today there are over 18 million teenagers in this country.

2. In part because of their numbers, but in addition because of their influence on the total culture, teenagers,

if not always listened to, are certainly being watched. The culture of this country is based on youth, and unprecedented studies are being conducted to understand the habits and norms of young people. Teenagers are being studied carefully, and that in itself may account for a more accurate account of what teenagers are doing in relation to alcohol.

Certainly it is rare to find anyone who has not had at least one drink before entering high school. In New York City over the last four years, there has been a 48% increase in the number of 15-year-olds who had their first drink before the seventh grade. While one drink may not seem terribly important, keep in mind that government and private studies show a trend toward increased alcohol use by adolescents. Teenagers are therefore taking their first drinks at an earlier age than ever before. They are also drinking more frequently in significant amounts for longer periods of time.

Depending on who you are and where you live, how much and how often you drink can vary greatly. There are any number of contradictory standards as to what is acceptable drinking behavior in regard to frequency and amount. You probably know someone who thinks nothing of having a beer or two at the beginning and end of each school day. Perhaps as important, his or her parents may not feel that this is excessive drinking. There are even differences of opinion as to what constitutes a light or heavy drinker. We took a poll of 500 students and came up with these definitions. Perhaps you may wish to test yourself or friends as to how much and how often you drink.

Myself	Others	Definition
		Abstainer: Does not drink at all.
		Infrequent Drinker: One drink a month at most; perhaps a toast or a small amount at an infrequent social occasion.
		Light Drinker: One to four drinks per month of small quantities.
		Moderate Drinker: One drink per week of small quantity; luncheon cocktail, etc.
		Moderate/Heavy Drinker: One or two drinks per day; heavy quantity at party.
		Heavy Drinker: Three or more drinks per day; heavy amounts per social occasion. Feels need to drink.
		Buzz Head: Heavy drinking every day; likes to get high off liquor.

2 Alcoholism in America: The Real Deal

ALCOHOLISM IN AMERICA is an insidious problem that pervades all levels of our society. It is estimated that there are 9.3 to 10 million problem drinkers, which represent 7% of the 145 million adult population. It is further estimated that there are 3.3 million young people who have problems with alcohol. This represents 14% of the 17 million persons between the ages of 14 and 17.

Alcohol abuse is a difficult issue to present because of the dichotomy with which it is treated in our society. While it is generally legal to drink at any age throughout the United States, it is usually illegal to purchase alcoholic beverages when you are under 18. But, as previously mentioned, you don't have to look hard for reasons to drink socially in this country because alcohol is part of the majority of American celebrations. It is therefore difficult to be taken seriously when discussing alcohol with young people, for they frequently retort, "Well, you drink," or "Everyone drinks."

Following are some astounding facts about alcohol. Though we are aware that statistics can often be boring, we feel that you may be surprised to find that some may apply to a number of people you know.

General

We often look upon alcoholism as something that could never happen to us. The statistics given here, from the National Council on Alcoholism, are not meant to frighten you, but to show how significant an impact alcohol can have on someone like *yourself*.

1. Two-thirds of the U.S. population are drinkers. Of the remaining one-third who abstain, 50% at one time were drinkers.

2. Skid-row drinkers represent only 3% to 5% of all U.S. alcoholics; the remainder are ordinary people.

3. Of the adults who drink, 36% can be classified as problem drinkers or as having potential problems with alcohol (10% and 26%, respectively).

4. It is estimated that alcohol-related deaths may run as high as 205,000 per year, or 11% of the 1.9 million deaths in 1975. Studies have shown that alcohol was involved in 40% of fatal industrial accidents, 69% of drownings, 83% of fire fatalities, and 70% of fatal falls.

5. Recent evidence suggests that social drinking impairs intellectual capacities. When tested on cognitive tests in the sober state, people who reported drinking more alcohol had poorer performance than lighter drinkers.

6. The average alcoholic is a man or woman in the middle 30s with a good job, a good home, and a family.

7. Those who drink or who drink excessively cross all

racial, social, and sexual boundaries. Alcoholism affects everyday people.

Teenagers

The problem begins early and, if we are not careful, can have long-range effects.

1. Problem drinking increases from 5% in the seventh grade to 40% in the twelfth grade for boys, and from 4% in the seventh grade to 21% in the twelfth grade for girls.

2. Of delinquents, 30% to 40% come from alcoholic homes. Of problems brought to Family Court, 40% are alcohol-related.

3 The proportion of teenagers reported to be intoxicated at least once a month rose from 10% in 1966 to 19% in 1975.

4. Over the last four years there has been a 48% increase in the number of 15-year-olds who had their first drink before the seventh grade.

5. The proportion of high school students who reported having been drunk increased dramatically from 19% before 1966 to 45% between 1966 and 1975.

Special Groups

Sly Stone used to sing "Different strokes for different folks." Whatever the reason, whatever the race or nationality, alcoholism affects "everyday people."

1. Up to 10% of the elderly male population are problem drinkers, and approximately 10% of alcoholics in treatment are 60 years or older. Only 2% of the elderly in general are problem drinkers.

2. Among black males the rates of both moderate drinking and heavier drinking are slightly less than for white males.

3. A smaller proportion of black females who do drink have a greater proportion of heavier drinkers.

4. Among all special population groups in the United States, American Indians have the highest reported frequency of problems associated with drinking.

Women

The issues connected with being a woman today are complex. To cope with life's hurdles, teenage women need to actively explore and clarify who they are in this society, rather than use alcohol as a substitute for the self-exploration that can result in personal power.

1. It is conservatively estimated that the number of adult women with alcohol problems ranges from 1.5 to 2.5 million.

2. Studies show that, *regardless of their lifestyle,* women drink primarily in relation to life crises, and to relieve loneliness, inferiority feelings, and conflicts about their sex roles.

3. The woman alcoholic is left by 9 out of 10 husbands, whereas 9 out of 10 wives stay with the male alcoholic.

4. A woman tends to drink at home—alone. Nearly 60% of American women are still employed primarily in the home; a woman, therefore, is less likely than a man to be identified as a problem drinker by an employer or co-worker and receive help through a job-related program.

5. If a woman alcoholic has a family, her husband and children are more likely to "protect" her—and themselves—from public exposure, instead of encouraging her to seek help.

6. Women alcoholics are more likely to become involved with other drugs (e.g., tranquilizers).

7. The incidence of alcoholism among divorced women is far greater than that found in the average population.

8. Alcoholism is a major factor in 20% of all divorces in New York City.

9. The criminal justice system, through which alcoholic men are often identified and assisted, tends to look the other way when confronted by a woman with a drinking problem—nationally, DWI and Driver Education and Referral programs break down to 85% male and 15% female.

10. Studies now show that just as many teenage females drink as do adolescent males.

Pregnant Women

A woman who drinks heavily during pregnancy runs the risk of permanent damage to her child. The result of heavy alcohol consumption during pregnancy is called Fetal Alcohol Syndrome (FAS).

The manifestations of FAS show up in the child in some or all of the following ways, depending on the extent, duration, and timing of alcohol abuse:

1. Growth deficiencies: Child is smaller than normal, both when born and during infancy.

2. Microcephaly (abnormally small head).

3. Reduced intellectual performance (may be borderline retarded).

4. Facial and head abnormalities.

5. Joint abnormalities.

6. Heart defects.

7. Brain abnormalities.

8. Genital anomalies.

Workers

Most teenagers, still developing vocationally, are not "locked" in their jobs. Drinking on the job is not fun or funny, however, and it can lead to serious and often dangerous consequences.

1. Nationally, an average of 6% of all employees suffer from alcoholism. Conservatively estimated, each alcoholic employee costs his/her company 25% of his/her salary.

2. The annual cost of alcoholism to American industry is approximately $20 billion.

3. The alcoholic employee is absent *2 to 4 times more frequently* than non-alcoholic employees. *Off-the-job accidents are 4 to 6 times as numerous.*

4. Sickness and accident benefits paid out for alcoholic employees are *3 times greater* than for the average non-alcoholic employee.

Crime, Mental Illness, and Suicide

The effect that alcohol has on one's self-control can be devastating. Teenagers who abuse alcohol often become "someone else" under its influence.

I started drinking heavily two years ago. I went to the Forum, here in Los Angeles, to see the Stones. My sister and her friends let me hang out because I looked mature. Well, everybody was drinking and smoking and I must have had about four cans of beer and some wine. I was like a different person. I could really be myself, you know.

Carole, 16

1. Studies have shown that when male social drinkers drink in a group situation with peers or friends, interpersonal aggressions increase significantly. (Think about your last attendance at a large rock concert, the liquor consumed, and the "macho" behavior.)

2. Of all police arrests, 50% are alcohol-related.

3. Alcohol is a contributing factor in more than 50% of all homicides.

4. Of all male admissions to state mental hospitals, 40% are alcoholics.

5. More than one-third of all suicides involve alcohol, and a disproportionately high number of people with drinking problems kill themselves. In 1975 as many as 10,000 suicides were alcohol-related, and up to 8,400 were committed by alcoholics.

Driving

Not only isn't it adult-like to drink and drive, it isn't smart either.

1. Of all fatal accidents occurring on the roads today, 50% involve alcohol. That represents 30,000 highway deaths.

2. One-third of all traffic injuries are alcohol-related, according to current estimates.

A surefire formula for not reaching adulthood—

Alcohol + Automobile = Termination

3 Why Are Teens Drinking?

THERE ARE MANY THEORIES that attempt to explain why teenagers drink. One researcher, George Globetti, Professor of Sociology at the University of Alabama (1964, 1974), points out that many teenagers who drink heavily have parents who strongly disapprove of their drinking, although the parents themselves drink. The teenagers' drinking was a form of rebellion and was almost always concealed.

Another theory, which we adhere to, is the "peer-pressure" theory. Simply, the peer-pressure theory argues that much of teenage drinking results from a desire to gain acceptance. Being accepted by the group or clique is of utmost importance to most teenagers, and consequently many are pressured or seduced into drinking. However, if young people have a strong sense of self-esteem and the necessary support system, they may avoid this trap. But if you are a teenager, be aware that saying no to your friends may be a very difficult and painful experience.

Many teenagers are drinking earlier merely because of the behavior to which they are most exposed. Fortunately for some, their parents still have an immeasurable positive influence on them. Having parents who don't drink or who teach their children how to be responsible drinkers will probably greatly reduce the chances of those teenagers abusing alcohol.

For many teenagers, drinking and smoking represent symbols of approaching adulthood. In much the same way that many of us imitated our parents by dressing up in their clothes, many teenagers begin to drink in order to feel "grown-up." When asked why they drank, many young people we talked to responded by saying, "I drink to feel good" or "to hang out." While these were the most common reasons, others were: "To be cool"—which we felt implied their desire to be adult and to be accepted; and "to deal"—that is, to cope—with school, family, and social pressures. In fact, few of the teenagers we talked to drank to get drunk. Drinking more often than not took place in groups of varying sizes and rarely did we find groups who were self-destructive. True, no one knows for certain why teenagers are increasingly abusing alcohol; but we do know that the two greatest influences on adolescents are their peers and their parents.

The authors' grandmothers, Mrs. Mary Johnson and Mrs. Ola Diggs, believed that it was always the parents' fault if any child, and especially their grandchildren, did something wrong. As a result, they would criticize our mothers if we misbehaved. This wisdom of our grandmothers should be applied to America, for though teenage drinking can be viewed as part of the growing-up process, alcohol abuse by teenagers can be regarded as evidence of a failure of society and, in particular, of the family.

As America has become increasingly technological, the

demands placed on the family unit have been overwhelming, forcing adjustments in the entire manner in which it functions. Specifically, there has been a delegation of many family responsibilities to institutions, especially to the schools and other community agencies.

Though nearly everyone recognizes and accepts the diminished role of the family, there has never been a really hard look taken at what the changes in the family have meant or what their impact has been. Indeed, the real nature of the changes has not yet been formulated, so it is not clear whether the institutions, specifically the schools, have accepted the family-relinquished tasks as part of their mission. Herein lies the crucial problem that is confronting many adolescents: They are missing a critical part of the parenting essential to their self-actualization. A recovered teenage alcoholic who began drinking at age 13 comments:

I think I may have begun to drink because no one cared about me and I sure didn't care about myself. Both of my parents worked two jobs and were always tired. The teachers in school were too busy and well, I just slipped into getting high. I had to learn about myself, and care about myself, before I could get my life together.

Think for a moment of the individual who has meant the most to you. Chances are you were influenced by his or her behavior. There is also a good chance that that person was a member of your family. But many teenagers are forced to develop their own families, because their nuclear families are disintegrating. Gangs, cults, and social clubs frequently take the place of disintegrating nuclear families, and from these groups the teenagers' values and attitudes are learned.

The Forces on the Family

The American family is faced with many forces that are causing changes. These include:

1. The need for both parents to work in order to earn enough money to allow them to have even a modest lifestyle.

2. Inflation is forcing parents to work harder and longer hours to maintain the status quo.

3. Society is constantly changing technologically, imposing daily demands to respond to the changes.

4. There is a bombardment of information, making parents insecure in their own knowledge; as a result they feel incompetent as educators and as purveyors of facts.

5. The media—a discussion of which concludes this chapter.

The bottom line of the changes is that the amount of time parents have to interact with their children is significantly reduced. They are no longer teaching their teenagers the skills and values that would adequately prepare them for life, so the young people are forced to learn the skills and values necessary for survival in the streets. When this happens, teenagers frequently learn to "get high" in order to cope.

The Media Hype

We cannot discount the impact of the media, not only on the general population, but on family life and, consequently, on teenagers. Television in particular has become a focal point of family activities and entertainment, and has grown so powerful that many of us simply no longer have to think for ourselves. With families strapped by very real pressures, television and the slick radio stations catering to adolescents through music have assumed the new responsibility of determining what is important and what isn't. After all, why would you want to be like your parents or teacher when you are faced with the image of a tall, lean cowboy who, through tight lips and a squint, orders a beer from an intimidated bartender who gives him one befitting his image? As one teenager commented, in a group session on alcohol and the media:

Hey, with these commercials, they're all my heroes. If you never wanted to drink before, when you get finished with that slick stuff, you'll stay blasted.

Since most of us would love to be as attractive as the models we see on television and can be manipulated into fantasizing about drinking the same things they do, it is not difficult to understand why impressionable teenagers are tempted into imitating them. The beer and wine industries spend millions of dollars enticing viewers to drink their products; the hard-liquor industry spends comparable amounts advertising its wares in newspapers and magazines, on billboards, and the like. We can only hope that, to counteract the damaging influence of such commercials and advertisements, someone (maybe one of our readers?) will initiate a creative campaign to *discourage* teenagers from drinking.

We still don't know why many teenagers drink, but we trust we have alerted you to a number of possibilities concerning this very serious problem. How do we—adults and teenagers alike—help those who have a drinking problem? How we help ourselves so that we can help others is what the remainder of this book is all about.

4 Where Are Teens Drinking?

WE'VE TALKED about why teenagers are drinking. But where do they drink? What are some of the hangouts they use? We will explore a few in this chapter.

For the most part, drinking is not sanctioned by adults. Of course, there are occasions when adults may look the other way or even approve of teenagers drinking—for example, at holiday gatherings and wedding celebrations— but these situations occur in traditional social settings and are generally controlled. When teenagers usually drink, however, it is in an atmosphere of "Let's hurry up so we don't get caught."

As a result, some teenagers can be ingenious at finding places to get high. Rooftops, hallways, and bathrooms are favorite places during school hours. One Chicago high school student told us:

19

We had it down to a science. We would take turns coming to school a period early. We would mostly get beer and hide it in the tanks of the toilets on the third floor. By the fourth period, the beer would be nice and cold and we would down it between periods for the rest of the day. The teachers could sometimes smell the beer on our breaths, but they could never figure out when we were doing it, or how.

Terry, 17

One real danger in this surreptitious drinking is that, because speed is often essential, teenagers gulp their liquor. Consequently, large doses of alcohol are passed rapidly into the bloodstream, and this causes drunkenness.

In checking with teenagers about where they did their drinking, we came up with the following favorite "watering holes":

1. Schoolyards and athletic fields (check for bottles and cans under the stands).

2. Clubhouses—usually managed by young adults or gangs or adults who profit off teenagers by selling them drugs, etc.

3. Home, at parties thrown during school hours while parents are working; this is called "shacking," or "busting the crib."

4. Cars—cruising and drinking and hoping the high wears off by the time you have to go home.

Drinking is a part of our way of life and, if done responsibly, can be enjoyable for most people. If you are a drinking teenager who has your own favorite hiding place where you get high with others in your peer group, perhaps the question you should ask yourself is, "Does downing my liquor in hiding allow me to be the kind of person I want to be?"

5 How You Get Hooked

IF YOU ARE A YOUNG MAN OR WOMAN in your teens, you are probably aware that the majority of your peers, almost 60%, have used or will use alcohol in some form before they leave high school. Of course, "use" can mean anything from a single drink or a taste of someone else's drink to fairly regular weekend drinking parties.

We talked earlier, in terms of family, school, and peer pressure, about why many teenagers drink. But how does a kid who has few of these pressures get hooked on alcohol? Are there other reasons for teenagers getting high? Some of the teenagers we talked to replied in these ways:

I like to get high. It's that simple. I like the feeling I get, like nothing bothers me, you know, and I feel I can deal with anything or anyone. A couple of beers or some wine and some reefer and I'm ready for the day.

Tony, 15—New York City

I drink because it's cheap and it helps me when I get bored.

Sharon, 15—Los Angeles

We always get high. Everybody around here has always gotten high—why shouldn't we?

Pete, 18—Chicago

To repeat, most teenagers do not set out to get drunk when they drink. However, if a teenager is having difficulty coping with family, school, or peer pressure, alcohol can offer a quick and often dangerous escape from stress. When his or her drinking reaches a stage where it becomes a continuing problem in any department of his or her life, then the teenager is alcoholic.

There may be patterns to a teenager's road to alcoholism. Here are some that we have observed in our work:

He or she

—begins to drink more than the other members of the group.

—begins to drink on more frequent occasions than his or her peers.

—behaves, when drinking, in a way that goes beyond what the peer group considers normal.

—begins to experience "blackouts" or temporary amnesia during and following drinking episodes.

—drinks more rapidly than others.

—drinks secretly.

—begins to lose control of the time, place, and amount of drinking, and drinks—and often gets unintentionally drunk—at inappropriate times and places.

—hides and protects a supply of liquor so as never to be caught short.

—drinks to overcome the hangover effects of prior drinking.

—tries new patterns of drinking in terms of time, place, amounts, and type of drinks.

—attempts cures by moving to new locations or seeking out different drinking groups.

—becomes a "loner" in his or her drinking sessions, and ingestion of alcohol becomes the sole purpose of drinking.

—develops an elaborate system of lies, alibis, excuses, and rationalizations to cover up or explain his or her drinking.

—undergoes personality and behavioral changes which adversely affect the family situation, friendship groups, or on-the-job relationships. Incurs accidents, job losses, family quarrels, broken friendships, and trouble with the law even when not under the influence of alcohol.

Manifestations of the final phases of alcoholism are obvious and tragic: extended binges; physical tremors; hallucinations and deliria; complete rejection of social reality; malnutrition, with accompanying illnesses—and an early death if the disease isn't treated. It should be pointed out that these deteriorating effects appear gradually, but with increasing frequency and intensity, over a period of years. This is why the disease is referred to as "progressive" and why it is generally described according to the stages of development—i.e., first-stage, middle-stage, and third-stage alcoholism. During this progression of the illness, the drinker's deviations from normal behavior multiply and deepen in the following ways:

First Stage

1. Makes promises to quit drinking and then breaks them.
2. Drinks to relieve tension.
3. Develops an increasing tolerance to alcohol.
4. Becomes irritable and forgetful.

Middle Stage

1. Tries to deny or conceal drinking.
2. Drinks in the morning and alone.
3. Finds drinking has become a daily necessity.
4. Needs an increased quantity of alcohol to feel good.

Final Stage

1. Becomes isolated from friends and family, and generally feels guilty.
2. Undergoes personality changes.
3. Lives to drink—does not eat.
4. Experiences "the shakes" and hallucinations.

At any of these stages, the drinker has developed a serious and complex illness from which he or she cannot recover without help. It is no longer a question of choice or of willpower, for he or she has neither, as far as the use of alcohol is concerned. Fortunately, however, the condition is treatable and, like other diseases, the earlier it is properly diagnosed and treated, the speedier and more effective will be the recovery. And the recovery rate is high, ranging up to 80% of those undergoing treatment.

In the next chapter, we will discuss what alcohol is and the effects its abuse can have on your body.

6 Alcohol and Your Body

Alcohol Content of Liquor

The alcohol content of liquor is measured in terms of "*proof.*"* Essentially, proof is twice the percentage of alcohol in a liquor. A 100-proof contains 50% alcohol.

For example, if you drink 2 ounces of 100-proof liquor, you are drinking 1 ounce of alcohol. If you drink 12 ounces of a 10-proof beer, you are drinking .60 ounces of alcohol.

---

* The term *proof* comes from 17th-century England, where it was used to designate the concentration of alcohol by volume. Liquor poured over gunpowder still allowed the gunpowder to ignite. Therefore, any liquor with an alcohol concentration of 57.35% by volume was termed *proof spirits.* Any under 57.35% alcohol was termed *underproof;* and more than 57.35%, *overproof.*

25

Type of Liquor	% Alcohol	Proof
Beer	4–6	8–12
Wine	10–12	20–24
Whiskey (rum, Scotch, gin, vodka	40–50	80–100
Overproof rum	75	151
Dessert wines, sherries, etc.	17–20	34–40
Liqueurs	20–50	40–100

Metabolism of Alcohol

Alcohol is not digested in the stomach and small intestines as is other "food," with enzymes breaking up carbohydrate and protein molecules into their basic components. Alcohol is absorbed directly through the stomach wall into the bloodstream.

The speed with which alcohol enters the bloodstream and exerts an effect on the brain, making the drinker high or drunk, depends on:

1. Speed of Drinking

The faster one drinks, the faster the blood alcohol level (see pp. 29–30) increases and as a result the faster one gets high. If you sip or nurse your drink, blood alcohol levels will remain lower.

2. Body Weight

The heavier a person is in terms of muscle, not fat, the lower will be his blood alcohol concentration (see pp. 29, 30–31). For example, a 200-pound man drinking 4 ounces of whiskey will have a blood alcohol concentration about one-half that of a man weighing 100 pounds.

3. Eating and Drinking

Eating when drinking slows the rate of absorption of alcohol into the bloodstream. This is not to be confused with metabolism. The body can still metabolize only one drink per hour. Food simply slows the amount of alcohol moving from the stomach into the bloodstream and, as a result, the amount of alcohol in the blood is lower.

4. Body Chemistry and Drinking History

Each person has an individual pattern of response to alcohol. If one's stomach tends to empty more rapidly, the effect of alcohol will be felt more rapidly. Persons with a long history of drinking tend to have a greater tolerance (can drink more without feeling the effects) to alcohol. As a result they need far more alcohol to get high or drunk.

5. Type of Beverage

The basic ingredient in liquors is alcohol; however, in addition to the alcohol there are other ingredients—those which give the liquor its flavor, as well as mixers—which affect the rate at which alcohol is absorbed or metabolized.

Also
—wine and beer tend to be absorbed more slowly than other liquors.

—alcohol diluted with water slows absorption.

—alcohol mixed with carbonated beverages increases absorption.

—aspirin slows absorption of alcohol.

—insulin in doses which cause hypoglycemia accelerates absorption because it causes gastric emptying.

Once in the bloodstream, alcohol travels to the liver, where it is metabolized through a process of oxidation. The key factor in this oxidation process is an enzyme called "alcohol dehydrogenase," which converts alcohol to acetaldehyde and releases one atom of hydrogen. The acetaldehyde is then converted by aldehydehydrogenase to acetyl coenzyme A, which then enters the normal metabolic process and produces energy.

The metabolism of alcohol produces 7 calories for each gram of alcohol. A standard 100-proof alcohol beverage contains 15 grams of alcohol, which produces 105 calories. One can of beer contains approximately the same amount of alcohol because of the other food products in beer which have higher caloric value.

What One Drink Per Hour Does to You

Alcohol is often thought to be a stimulant and, in low concentrations, does stimulate cellular activity. In moderate quantities it also increases heart rate, dilates blood vessels, lowers blood pressure moderately, stimulates appetite, increases the production of gastric juices, and stimulates urine output.

However, the general effect of alcohol on the body is that of a depressant, specifically on the central nervous system.

As we have pointed out, the effect alcohol has on an

individual depends on many factors. It is therefore foolish to think that you can drink as much as the next guy. The bottom line on drinking is that the body can metabolize and eliminate about 7 grams (½ ounce) of pure alcohol per hour. This amounts to *one drink per hour.* The following chart shows what "one drink" means in terms of various drinks:

1 shot 1½ oz of 80-proof liquor	5 oz regular wine*	12-oz can of beer	1 highball 1½ oz liquor
times	*times*	*times*	*times*
percent alcohol (40%)	percent alcohol (12%)	percent alcohol (5%)	percent alcohol (40%)
equals	*equals*	*equals*	*equals*
.60 oz alcohol	.60 oz alcohol	.60 oz alcohol	.60 oz alcohol

* For port or sherry, 3 oz. is the equivalent of 5 oz. regular wine.

In its general effect on the body as a depressant, alcohol decreases central-nervous-system activities in proportion to the concentration of alcohol in the blood, which is measured in terms of blood alcohol level (BAL) or blood alcohol concentration (BAC). The BAC is the percentage of alcohol per unit of blood.

Blood Alcohol Level (BAL)

Though different people respond differently to alcohol, the chart on page 30 illustrates the usual reaction.

Legally, in every state except Utah and Idaho (which use .08 as an indicator), one is considered intoxicated when the BAL reaches .10, which represents about 5 ounces of alcohol drunk in a period of one hour.

Quantity of alcohol	% BAL	Reaction
1.5 oz	.03	Excited
3 oz	.05	Sedated or tranquilized
6 oz	.10	Lack of coordination
12 oz	.20	Obvious intoxication
15 oz	.30	Unconsciousness
30 oz	.50+	Possible death

Opposite is a chart which computes the predicted BAC, based on the quantity drunk, the number of hours spent drinking, and weight.

With the BAC Chart, you can determine: (1) how different numbers of drinks affect your BAC, (2) how time affects your BAC after a specific number of drinks, and (3) how to limit drinking during different time periods to keep from being affected, impaired or intoxicated.

Using the BAC chart is a way to determine when you have had enough to drink. You should look at your weight and determine what pattern of drinking will enable you to remain sober. For example, if you weigh 150 lbs. you can probably have one drink per hour and remain sober and in control.

At a BAC of .01–.04% behavior is affected in terms of judgment, one is less critical, reaction time is slow, and one is more mentally relaxed.

At a BAC of .05–.09% judgment is not sound, thinking and reasoning powers not clear, ability to do complex jobs is lessened.

BAC CHART

After Hours	1 Drink				2 Drinks				3 Drinks				4 Drinks			
	4	3	2	1	4	3	2	1	4	3	2	1	4	3	2	1
Weight (lbs.)																
80	—	—	—	.02	—	—	.05	.08	.07	.10	.10	.10	.12	.12	.15	.15
100	—	—	—	.02	—	—	.04	.06	.05	.07	.08	.09	.09	.10	.12	.13
120	—	—	—	.02	—	—	.03	.04	.03	.04	.06	.08	.06	.08	.09	.11
140	—	—	—	.01	—	—	.02	.04	.02	.03	.05	.06	.04	.06	.08	.09
160	—	—	—	.01	—	—	.02	.03	.01	.02	.04	.05	.03	.04	.06	.08
180	—	—	—	.01	—	—	.01	.03	—	.02	.03	.04	.02	.04	.05	.07
200	—	—	—	—	—	—	.01	.02	—	.01	.03	.04	.01	.03	.04	.06

After Hours	5 Drinks				6 Drinks				7 Drinks				8 Drinks			
	4	3	2	1	4	3	2	1	4	3	2	1	4	3	2	1
Weight (lbs.)																
80	.17	.17	.19	.20	.19	.22	.22	.25	.25	.27	.27	.30	.29	.30	.32	.33
100	.13	.14	.16	.17	.16	.18	.19	.21	.20	.22	.23	.25	.24	.25	.27	.28
120	.09	.11	.13	.14	.13	.14	.16	.17	.15	.17	.19	.20	.19	.20	.22	.23
140	.07	.09	.10	.12	.10	.12	.13	.15	.13	.14	.16	.17	.15	.17	.18	.20
160	.06	.07	.09	.10	.08	.09	.11	.13	.10	.12	.13	.15	.13	.14	.16	.17
180	.04	.06	.07	.09	.06	.08	.09	.11	.09	.10	.12	.13	.11	.12	.14	.15
200	.03	.04	.06	.08	.05	.07	.08	.09	.07	.09	.10	.12	.09	.10	.12	.13

Numbers equal the percentage of alcohol in the blood. Dash (—) = a trace of alcohol.

At a BAC of .10%—intoxication—one cannot do simple tasks and reasoning power is severely impaired.

Alcohol's Effects on Various Parts of the Body

You probably thought that the primary effect of alcohol abuse was on the liver. It is true that liver cirrhosis still ranks as the sixth most common cause of death in the

United States, with 90% of those cases estimated to be alcohol-related. But did you also know that alcohol has been indisputably linked with the causation of cancer at various sites in the body? And drinking combined with smoking greatly increases the potential for developing cancer of the mouth, tongue, pharynx, larynx, esophagus,* and liver. It has also been shown that, aside from alcohol, the other chemicals in liquors may be carcinogenic (cancer-causing).

Here are how bodily organs and systems can be affected by alcohol:

Esophagus

Alcohol's impact on the esophagus results from either direct irritation of the lining; inducement of severe vomiting, which tears the lining; or impairment of movement, which causes gastric juices to back up into the esophagus. The result is the same in all these cases—bleeding, difficulty in swallowing, and pain.

Stomach

Alcohol has been implicated as the causative agent in stomach inflammation and bleeding lesions. The exact mechanism is not known but is believed to be the result of direct irritation by the alcohol or of the action of gastric juices which alcohol stimulates.

Small Intestine

Alcohol's effect on the small intestines involves two factors: the movements of the small intestine, and the ab-

---

* The risk of cancer of the esophagus (throat) is 5 times greater in smokers, 18 times greater in heavy drinkers, and 44 *times greater in persons who both drink and smoke.*

sorption of various vitamins, carbohydrates, and proteins. The alteration in intestine mobility results in food being propelled unimpeded through the intestines; the result is diarrhea.

Alcohol tends to impair the absorption of calcium, thiamine, iron, Vitamin B_{12}, and certain amino acids.

Pancreas

Chronic alcohol abuse is associated with inflammation of the pancreas. Acute alcohol abuse can interfere with the secretion of pancreas-produced digestive juices, which may cause the absorption abnormalities in the small intestine noted above.

Liver

The liver is one of the most complex organs in the body. It is involved in circulation, excretion, immunology, metabolism, and detoxification.

The most devastating result of alcohol abuse is cirrhosis of the liver, which is an inflammatory disease that causes replacement of liver cells with scar tissue. It was once thought that malnutrition resulting from alcohol abuse or alcoholism was the primary cause of cirrhosis, but it has since been shown that cirrhosis can be induced by even moderate alcohol use.

Metabolism

Alcohol affects the body metabolism in a number of ways:

1. Heavy alcohol ingestion causes ketoacidosis, which is an elevated level of blood acidity brought about by certain hormones releasing stored fatty acids. The fatty acids

are broken down, causing a buildup of intermediary products that have a toxic effect.

2. Alcohol similarly inhibits the conversion of amino acids into protein such as albumin, transferrin, and others important to blood coagulation.

3. Alcohol stimulates the production of lipo protein, which transports fat in the blood. The alteration in fat metabolism may result in a condition known as "fatty liver," which can cause death, especially in young people.

Nervous System

Alcohol is classified with a number of other drugs as a central-nervous-system depressant. Specifically, alcohol tends to affect the membrane of nerves, so that once a nerve has fired, alcohol reduces its ability to refire. As the concentration of alcohol is increased, the nerve loses its ability to fire at all. The resultant stages are anesthesia, narcosis, coma, and death.

Another effect of alcohol on the nervous system is the development of dependence upon alcohol. Consequently, when alcohol is withheld, the withdrawal syndrome appears, and the biologic systems cannot react quickly enough.

Heart

Alcohol has a profound impact on the heart, from elevation of blood pressure to coronary heart disease.

Cardiomyopathy: Alcohol or its by-products have a toxic effect on the myocardium, resulting in shortness of breath, signs of congestive heart failure, abnormal heart signs, edema, heart enlargement, spleen and liver enlargement, and noisy breathing. This does not come on suddenly, but rather creeps up and is dependent upon the length and severity of drinking.

Coronary Heart Disease: Heavy drinking over a long period of time increases the possibility of coronary heart disease. The coronary arteries are the blood vessels that carry blood from the heart. Disease of the arteries increases the possibility of a heart attack. What is interesting is that moderate use of alcohol—up to 2.5 ounces—decreases the chances of heart attacks.

Cardiac Arrhythmias: Alcohol can cause irregular heartbeats. The excessive drinking that usually takes place during holidays causes irregular heartbeats in otherwise healthy persons. The occurrence is known as "holiday heart syndrome."

Blood Pressure: Alcohol use tends to elevate blood pressure in those persons consuming more than three drinks a day.

Metabolism in the Heart: Alcohol has been shown to cause damage to the heart-muscle mitochondria, which produces the energy to keep the heart beating.

Muscle System

Prolonged drinking can result in muscle weakness and atrophy. The disease is known as "alcoholic myopathy," which can be fatal.

Endocrine System

Gonads: Alcohol has been shown to cause sexual impotence; a reduction in the size of the testes; a decrease in the production of testosterone (the male hormone in the testes), which results in breast enlargement; loss of facial hair; and loss of sexual drive.

Pituitary: Alcohol inhibits the release of oxytocis, a hormone that causes the uterus and mammary glands to contract. This characteristic of alcohol has been used to inhibit premature labor.

The Hangover

Perhaps the most immediate result of irresponsible drinking is the hangover or "the morning after." The exact cause of hangovers is not known, and though they are of no immediate danger they can be very unpleasant.

We had been drinking rum and Coke at this party and I must of had four or five drinks. I was really feeling good. When we ran out of rum, we had something called a Harvey's Wallbanger. I have never been so sick in my life after mixing those drinks. But the morning after was worse. I thought my head would split open. Getting nice was cool, but I can't deal with those hangovers.

Cynthia, 18

There are no known remedies for hangovers, although many of you may have your own methods for dealing with the day after. Here are some of the more popular mythical treatments.

Vitamin preparations: Some people believe large doses of vitamins will help your body fight off the hangover. It isn't true.

Oxygen: Inhaling pure oxygen does not help your body oxidize the alcohol in your system. Your hangover, as a matter of fact, is due in part to your body oxidizing the alcohol. Put your scuba tank away.

Exercise: Your hangover will probably survive your morning jog better than you will.

Raw eggs: What was good for Rocky Balboa is no good for you on the morning after.

Tranquilizers: Double trouble—a definite no-no! (See Chapter 8.)

More alcohol: Today's cure may become tomorrow's problem.

Black coffee: It only works in the movies.

The big breakfast: It doesn't work and it's 7 to 5 you don't keep it down.

Ignore it: Your hangover will go away e-v-e-n-t-u-a-l-l-y.

You have probably heard about or tried some of these or other hangover cures. For some of you the remedies may help psychologically, but the best cure for hangovers is not to drink excessively. Hangovers can be prevented by drinking slowly, with food in the stomach, under relaxed social circumstances, and with restraint.

NO ONE EVER COMPLAINED OF HAVING ONE TOO FEW!

7 25 Myths and Rationalizations about Drinking

DESPITE FACTUAL KNOWLEDGE that tells us excessive drinking can be dangerous and even fatal, teenagers continue to drink. Many of you probably have favorite myths as well as rationales for your own drinking. We hope that after completing this section, which lists 25 of the most common ones, you will be able to separate fact from fiction.

1. *"Getting drunk is funny."*

Maybe watching Dean Martin play a drunk is funny to some, but being drunk is no laughing matter. There is about as much humor to alcoholism as there is to any other serious illness.

2. *"I'm friendlier when I'm drunk."*

Maybe. But, remember our earlier statistics, showing that one-half of all murders are alcohol-related, as are one-third of all suicides. People who are consistently drunk are more of everything that is destructive.

3. *"Alcohol is a stimulant."*

If being unconscious is stimulating, then this is the drug to choose. Alcohol, you'll recall, is a depressant on the central nervous system.

4. *"When you are really an alcoholic, the 'drunk tank' is the only cure for you."*

We don't put people in jail for tuberculosis or cancer. We don't, and shouldn't, put them in jail for alcoholism.

5. *"It's only beer."*

One beer or a glass of wine is equal to one highball of whiskey, vodka, or gin. The effect might be a little slower, but you will become just as drunk on beer as on "hard" liquor.

6. *"All that publicity about drinking and driving is exaggerated."*

We hope you don't try it. At least one-half of all fatal highway accidents are related to drinking.

7. *"Aw, come on, a few drinks can help you to unwind and relax."*

Maybe. But if you are consistently using alcohol as a medicine, it's time you saw a doctor.

8. *"What are ya worried about? At least I'm not on drugs."*

This is a case where ignorance isn't bliss. If you are hooked on drinking, you *are* hooked on drugs; so are millions of other people. Alcohol is a drug, and it's time we stopped pretending it isn't.

9. *"But my parents use it."*

The key here is *how* they use it. If they are using it responsibly, fine. If not, then what is your investment in being self-destructive?

10. *"I feel embarrassed telling my friend he has a drinking problem."*

Maybe if we weren't so self-conscious about our embarrassment, we wouldn't have so many friends with drinking problems.

11. *"Alcoholism is all in the mind."*
Sure, if you want to believe that 9 million people are just suffering from weak willpower. Alcoholism is a very real illness and there is scientific evidence that physiological dependence is involved.

12. *"Duke is my kind of man; he can really hold his liquor."*
Don't be so impressed. His ability to hold his liquor may be his body developing a tolerance for the drug, alcohol. And in case you don't realize it, tolerance is need.

13. *"Alcoholism isn't a problem in my community. In fact, I don't even know of any alcoholics."*
Most alcoholics try to hide their illness, even from themselves. A friend of yours could have a drinking problem and you could be unaware of it. Most alcoholics appear to be normal people, just like you and me. But if you are more worried about drug abuse, remember there are about 300,000 heroin addicts. Do you think one of these people might be someone you know?

14. *"People only get drunk from switching drinks."*
Switching usually doesn't make much of a difference. People generally get drunk from drinking too much.

15. *"My parents don't drink, so I won't become an alcoholic."*
Maybe. But the highest incidence of alcoholism occurs among children whose parents are either teetotalers or alcoholics. Perhaps the extremism of parents' attitudes is a significant factor. Education about drinking at an early age is still a sensible and intelligent approach for dealing with alcoholism.

16. *"What's the beef? People who drink only hurt themselves."*
Yeah—and their families, friends, teachers, employers, strangers at parties, people on the highway, etc., etc.

17. *"It's rude to refuse a drink."*

Baloney! It's rude to try and push drinks on someone who doesn't want them or on someone who shouldn't have them.

18. *"Very few women become alcoholic."*

Sorry, but alcoholism is an equal-opportunity disease. Women are afflicted with it just as much as men and have their own unique problems and circumstances.

19. *"My friend Tom is eighteen and he is a real man. He can down a fifth and still stay on his feet."*

Your friend is putting you on. Anyone who drinks a fifth of liquor in a couple of hours will probably be dead or in a hospital. There is nothing mature or "manly" about overdrinking. Would you be as impressed if he were overeating?

20. *"I have the best parties in school and I make sure my friends' glasses are never empty."*

We are not impressed. Do you also make sure your friends have full stomachs while they are drinking? How about investing that energy into ensuring that they have full lives by not pushing your values on others?

21. *"At my parties, the first round is a double to break the ice."*

Your task as host is to break the ice. Be a good host—break it with other things besides alcohol.

22. *"Indians can't drink."*

Some can, some can't, just as with people of any other nationality.

23. *"Jews don't drink."*

Some do, some don't.

24. *"Blacks can't hold their liquor."*

No more, no less than Jews, Catholics, Irish, Hispanics, etc., when alcohol is abused.

25. *"Never trust a kid who doesn't drink."*

The silliest myth of all. But people who don't drink often make those of us who do drink feel funny. Makes you wonder. . . .

8 Double Trouble— Alcohol and Other Drugs

ONE OF THE MOST DANGEROUS EFFECTS of alcohol is caused by mixing it with other drugs. The celebrated case of Karen Ann Quinlan points up this fact. Karen Ann was probably drinking and decided to take some sleeping pills (barbiturates). As a result she has been in a coma since 1976.

A general rule to follow is: Do not drink if you take pills. Following is a chart showing possible effects of combining alcohol and some specific drugs.

Some of the terms used in the chart are very technical, but keep in mind that there are some teenagers who drink while consuming downers, uppers, marijuana, or other drugs. Mixing alcohol with other drugs is like being in a chemistry class and fooling around with chemicals; you may inadvertently create a dangerous explosion.

ALCOHOL—DRUG INTERACTION*

Drugs Involved with Alcohol	Possible Effects and Clinical Significance
Narcotic pain killers (morphine, codeine, meperidine, methadone, etc.)	Acute ingestion—increased central nervous system depression and possible respiratory arrest. Well documented. Chronic ingestion—tolerance developed to depressant effects but not to effects on respiratory system.
Non-narcotic pain killers (aspirin and other related compounds)	Increased likelihood of gastrointestinal irritation with possibility of increased blood loss from gastrointestinal tract.
Anesthetics General anesthetics (thiamyial sodium, methohexital sodium, etc).	Additive central nervous system depressant effects in acute stage of intoxification.
Antialcohol preparations Disulfiram Calcium carbamide	Well-documented "antiabuse reaction" resulting in nausea, vomiting, headache, increased blood pressure, and possible severe cardiac arrhythmias. Can result in death.
Heart drugs Antianginal preparations Nitrates, nitrites, and other coronary vasodilators and peripheral vasodilators	Can produce an increased peripheral vasodilation and possible excessive lowering in blood pressure resulting in fainting, dizziness, or lightheadedness.

* Developed by the Texas Pharmaceutical Association.

Antidiabetic agents
Insulin, oral sulfinylureas (tolbutamide, tolazmide, acetohexamine, chlorproamide), phenformin

Alcohol can result in an indirect increase in the effects of insulin—may induce severe hypoglycemia. Alcohol inhibits gluconeogenesis and induces a hypoglycemia when this mechanism is needed to maintain normal glucose levels (i.e., inadequate carbohydrate reserves). It also inhabits the rebound of glucose after hypoglycemia. With the oral sulfonylureas, alcohol may stimulate their metabolism resulting in a decreased hypoglycemia activity. A possible disfiram-like effect may be produced in certain diabetics. With phenformin, a severe state of lactic acidosis may be produced with alcohol and should therefore be avoided.

Antihistamines
Ethylendiamines (tripelennamine, methapyrilene, etc.)
Ethanolamines (diphenhydramine, dyphenylpryaline, etc.)
Propylamines (brompheniramine maleate, chlorpheniramine maleate, triprolidine HCl, etc.),
Phenothiazines (promethazine, etc).

Increased sedative effects with the combination but will vary with the class of antihistamine.

High blood pressure agents
Rauwolfa alkaloids (reserpine, deserpidine, etc.) Guanethidine, Alpha-methylodopa, ganglionic

An increase in the blood pressure lowering effects may be noted with this combination with the possibility of producing postural hypotension. Additionally, an increased central nervous system depressant effect may be seen with the rauwolfa alkaloids and alpha-methyldopa.

blocking agents (mecalyamine, etc.), Hydralazine, pargyline

Anticoagulants
Enolic (bishydroxycoumarin, warfarin sodium, phenprocoumom, acenocoumarol, Indanediones (phenindione, anisindione, diphenadione)

Alcohol may decrease the anticoagulant's effects through enzymatic stimulation. Alcohol may also decrease liver function when consumed chronically and may lead to a decreased clotting factor synthesis.

Anticonvulsants
Diphenylhydantoin

The anticonvulsant activity of diphenylhydantoin has been reported to be decreased through enzymatic stimulation by alcohol.

Antidepressants
Tricyclic (imipramine, desipramine, norpramine, amitriptyline, protrityline)
Doxepin
Monamine oxidase inhibitors (tranylcypromine, nialamide, phenelazine, isocarbozazid, pargyline)

With the tricyclic antidepressants and doxepin, increases central nervous system depression. Alcohol may also adversely affect motor skills, particularly during the first few days of tricyclic antidepressant therapy. With the monoamine oxidase inhibitors, increases sedative effects with a possibility of a disfram-like effect. Certain alcohol preparations (Chianti wine, in particular) may also be responsible for precipitating a hypertensive crisis.

Antiinfective agents
Sulfonamides
Metronidazole

Possible disulfiram-like effect
Possible disulfiram-like effect

Nitrofurans (furazolidone, nifurozime)

Possible disulfiram-like effect

Cycloserine

Possible precipitating of convulsions when combined with alcohol.

Central nervous system stimulants Amphetamines, caffeine, methylphenidate, etc.

Possible antagonism of central nervous system depressant effects of alcohol but no improvement of impaired motor coordination. May result in false sense of security.

Diuretics
Thiazide (chlorothiazide, hydrochlorothiazide, methychlorothiazide, etc.), Thiazide-like (chlorthalidone, quinethazone, etc.) Furosemide, Ethacrynic acid, etc.

May produce an increase in blood pressure lowering effects from the diuretics and may possibly precipitate postural hypotension.

Sedative-Hypnotics
Barbiturates (phenobarbital, pentobarbital, secobarbital, amobarbital, butabarbital, etc.) Non-barbiturates (gluthimide, chloral hydrate, chlorbetaine, methaqualone, ethchlorvynol, flurazepam, etc.), bromides

Combination can result in increased central nervous system depression with possible coma and respiratory arrest. Chronic alcohol consumption can produce a cross-tolerance to sedative effects but not to the respiratory depressive effects. Possible fatal results.

Tranquilizers

Minor (chlordiazepoxide, diazepam, oxazepam, meprobamate, tybamate, phenaglycodol, hydroxyzine, etc.)

Major (phenothiazines, etc.)

Increased central nervous system depression, particularly during the first few weeks of therapy with tranquilizers. Very well documented. Increased central nervous system depression with impairment of motor skills, particularly during first few weeks of therapy.

Vitamins

Cyanocobolamin (B12), Thiamine HCl (B1), Folic acid, Fat-soluble vitamins (A,D,E,K)

Chronic alcohol consumption can result in decreased absorption from gastrointestinal tract. Reversible when alcohol is withdrawn.

9 Dr. Bob Answers Questions about Drinking

THE QUESTIONS dealt with came from teenagers, parents, and teachers.

Dear Dr. Bob:

I am only 14. Aren't I too young to be an alcoholic?

Many teenagers associate alcoholism with middle age or the image of the derelict. Teenagers who are alcoholic rationalize their behavior by thinking, "It's just a bad habit." The fact is, alcoholism is a disease, like cancer, TB, or heart disease. It strikes at any age, irrespective of sex, race, or social background. Remember, also, that teenagers are taking their first drinks earlier than ever, so presumably they may be drinking longer.

Dear Dr. Bob:

If I stop drinking at 14 (now), will I be missing my most fun-filled years?

Getting drunk is no fun and one sure way of not getting drunk is to abstain from drinking. If you are abusing alcohol, I can assure you that the years ahead will not be fun-filled. Contact your local Alcoholics Anonymous or Alateen and talk to some of the recovered alcoholics in reference to what you think you might be missing if you stop now.

Dear Dr. Bob:

Does drinking improve my sex life?

NO WAY. Physically it can have the opposite effect. The image of the "macho" drinking man taking his woman is strictly Hollywood. If you think drinking constantly lets the beast rise up inside of you, it may be that your problem is quite serious and you need to get help. By the way, drinking is bad for the breath also.

Dear Dr. Bob:

I don't touch anything stronger than beer. Is that OK?

Many of us rationalize our drinking by claiming we don't touch the hard stuff, only beer or wine. Consuming any alcoholic beverage in excess over a period of time can lead to alcoholism. It isn't the flavoring, the grain, or the grape. It isn't the bubbles or the water or even the brand name; it's the alcohol that causes trouble.

Dear Dr. Bob:

How can I tell if my friend is an alcoholic?

Here are some cues and clues that may help you.

1. Has your friend begun to be absent from school frequently?

2. Does your friend have recent money problems and is borrowing from peers?

3. Have your friend's grades slipped?

4. Does your friend complain about fainting or loss of memory?

5. Does your friend have to have a drink before going out on a date?
6. Has he or she lost friends recently?
7. Does your friend act differently at parties or social events after a couple of drinks?
8. Does he or she hang out with a crowd that drinks heavily?
9. What do your instincts tell you, as a friend?
10. Does he or she hide the fact that he/she is drinking?

If you answered yes to most of these questions, chances are your friend has a drinking problem.

Dear Dr. Bob:
My husband and I don't drink and my daughter wants to. What should I do?

Sit down and discuss your daughter's drinking the way you would any other family issue. Your daughter is probably responding to peer and societal pressure as well as her own curiosity. Share with her your concerns and negotiate some boundaries that are mutually agreed upon for her drinking: when and where and how much. If you approach the situation reasonably, if your years of training as a parent have been productive, your daughter will approach drinking intelligently and reasonably.

Dear Dr. Bob:
I like to drink and my girlfriend doesn't. Sometimes I get really high and I have to drive. I can't let anyone else drive my girl home.

Those Steve McQueen and Clint Eastwood movies where after three or four stiff drinks they jump into their cars and go after the bad guys are performed by stunt men. Get my drift? If you are drinking, then let her drive or allow a sober friend to drive. About 50% of all fatal auto accidents involve alcohol. Your machismo may suffer, but you'll live to talk about it.*

Dear Dr. Bob:

I don't like drinking, but my boyfriend does and I want to keep him. How do I say no when he tries to get me to drink?

A good solid relationship between people must have clear and open lines of communication, trust, and mutual respect. If your boyfriend cannot allow you your differences, then he is denying a part of who you are. Talk to him; if he cannot allow your individuality and right of choice, then chances are the relationship would not last long anyhow. If your instincts, values, and experience tell you not to drink—then don't drink, and find someone who will appreciate you for that.

Dear Dr. Bob:

How do I say no at a party when I am pressured to drink?

By saying it clearly, honestly, emphatically, and proudly; and by saying "Thank you" afterward.

---

* As the level of alcohol increases in the blood, the probability of a driving accident increases at a greater rate. For example, if you were to drive after having two drinks in one hour, your chances of an auto accident increase slightly. If you have three drinks in an hour, your chances of an accident double. Four drinks in an hour increase the chance of an accident by six times. Six drinks increase the chances of an accident twenty-five times.

10 Young People Tell Their Stories

HOW DO YOUNG PEOPLE in California feel about drinking? How about those in Chicago, Atlanta, and Detroit, as well as New York City? To find out, we conducted interviews with teenagers and young adults up to 21 years of age in airports, discotheques, bars, schools, community agencies, and on street corners throughout the country.

In this chapter we will give a sampling of the various replies we received to two of the several questions we asked of each, as well as the transcripts of two more lengthy question-and-answer interviews conducted at the Harbor for Young Men and Women. Also included are seven "case studies," of young people with whom we are still working. All names, of course, have been changed.

Interviews:

What were your experiences with alcohol as a teenager?
I started drinking rum and Coke around seventeen.
But it was always a little bit of rum or whatever whiskey
it was, and plenty of soft drink, because I wasn't into
drinking at all. I was afraid of it.

*

Well, as a teenager, you know, I experimented with alcohol like it was the big thing. After you'd start smoking
cigarettes, you know, you'd start drinking. Everybody . . .
all the guys hang out and see who could drink the most
beers and who could drink the strongest liquor and get
drunk and sick. . . .

*

I was an assistant counselor in a camp in Michigan one
summer—it was the summer after junior year and it had
been a great summer. The campers had just gone home
the day before and so the plan was to have a staff party
the whole next day. This was the first break we'd had in
nine weeks away from these damn kids. We're only fifteen, sixteen, but we were like supervising kids that lived
away from home in summer camp that were like our age
or under. And to make a long story short, I blew lunch
[vomited] on waterskis in the middle of Big Bass Lake.
. . . I was so drunk. I had all kind of fruit wines like Bali
Hai which is truly nasty—that used to be a big thing in
Chicago. . . . Bali Hai's like blueberry wine, all these
cheap wines.

*

I think I was against drinking from an early age because
I thought my father drank too much, although he wasn't

drunk and disorderly or anything like that. But I just always thought he drank too much.

*

One time in particular. . . . I was real . . . I was like bombed. You know, it was a Christmas Eve and my grandmother . . . came over and she like . . . she caught me. . . . I couldn't hide it, you know. Because when you're drunk you can't, you know. And she really . . . made me feel, you know, kind of bad . . . like I was an alcoholic and everything.

*

As a teenager . . . I didn't do too much drinking because . . . I couldn't develop a taste for alcohol for quite some time and like I would take maybe two or three drinks and I'm drunk and I'm climbing trees. . . .

*

Well, I didn't drink that much as a teenager. I had one bad experience drinkin' corn liquor and it shook me. . . .

*

I was eighteen, I remember that. Because in Illinois the legal age is twenty-one and we were going to a club one night and I had borrowed someone's ID so that I could get into the club. . . . We were coming from a BYOB party where I had consumed a lot of liquor, you know, a lot. In fact it was my first experience with being drunk. And I got to the club and the guy . . . knew the person whose ID I had and he refused to serve me. And it was a good thing. Because by that time I was so drunk. I went outside to wait for some friends in a little alleyway and I sat down there. And I was so drunk I fell asleep. I woke up like five hours later. The police were waking me up. I jumped in a taxi and went home. I didn't have my wallet. Told the cab driver to wait a minute, I would go in and get the money and went in the house. And my mother had, like, plastic runners on the floor and I slipped as soon as I walked in and I fell asleep and slept on the floor the whole night. And the next morning my mother . . . said, "There was a cab out front honking all night long." But I never told her why.

*

I went through the same thing that everybody else went through. You know, you grow up and you want to start drinking stuff like Malt Duck or Colt 45. . . . But when you get older you just say, "Later," and you stop. . . .

*

Well . . . I think most of the times that I drank, I drank because I was in a group. I drank because I was with friends and everybody else was drinking so I was drinking. When I was younger I never really got into marijuana or any other drugs. . . . I got into liquor before anything. Because it's a lot more accessible.

*

Minimal. As an adolescent at home my parents allowed us to get familiar with alcohol at an early age. We had wine, and if we wanted a drink, my mother would take a drop of Scotch and fill it up with water just so we got the thrill of drinking out of the way. It was never a big thing. . . .

Recalling your experience, what would you recommend, what type of advice, would you give teenagers today about alcohol?

Well, you know, I would recommend like stay away from it, like, there's no use for it, like, physically it's harming to the body. You know, mentally, you know you don't need it, it's just an external substance coming into the natural body . . . the body has no use for it and there's no purpose in its . . . you know, the people, corporations and individuals, you know, that are exploiting people—you know, the big whiskey industry—and there's really no need for the advertising campaigns. It's almost, you know . . . like a scandal the way a lot of these ads are thrown at young people and you know how specifically at black people . . . to buy these liquors and wines and stuff. So you know, my suggestion is just stay away from it, you know. Get to know yourself and use your own self and your values as a crutch instead of any other things like alcohol or drugs.

*

Well, I think that drinking is very harmful to people physically and mentally. . . . And people could really depend on alcohol. . . . in our neighborhood, you know, like we have . . . inner cities . . . Liquor stores and bars, you know, do tremendous business 'cause people from these areas they depend on alcohol; it's like an escape from their, you know, their cruel surrounding, so they . . . It's dangerous because people like sleep on their problems and they just rely on alcohol to get them through the days and the times.

Transcripts

The following are transcripts of two recent cases in which clients recount those critical incidents that prompted them to seek help.
Roger, age 17:
When did you begin drinking and why?
The first time I . . . well . . . my experiences with alcohol, drinking was always this common denominator be-

tween us, you know; and if you wanted to find out about a person or really get into something else, it was on an individual basis but you needed that line to tie a group together, you know, and when I started drinking I was thirteen, fourteen, you know, hanging out with the boys, and that was the common denominator, you know, whatever else jumped off from that, we'd get drunk to go out and party, we'd get drunk to go do this and that.

Could you elaborate on your adolescent experience with alcohol?

Oh, yeah, it was really wild. Really wild, because I remember a lot of crazy stuff I did to myself and others. But the first time I can really remember drinking was with these two guys who I recall from my elementary school years, one of them had liked my sister, but he was a couple of years behind her, this is from elementary school and I used to hang out at the roller skating rink. So this brother and another brother, who I didn't know at the time, met me there and we got to talking a little and what not. I was . . . I was what you call a nerd, you know, I mean, I was really . . . I was very sheltered, very bookish, you know. I hung out with kids around my block, you know, but that was about it. So this was one of my first times really hanging out. And one night the two of them came to my house and oh, they . . . one of them was trying to go out with a girl I knew, so that's how they connected themselves to me, but they came to my house and they said, "Claude, listen, we were supposed to be at a Yankee game tonight and we want to . . . can we, you know, take out the tube to see what the score is?" So they were checking out the score and at about eleven o'clock, they said, "Let's wait here 'til the game is over." So then they said, "At score such and such, let's go out and hang out." So this was a summer night, you know, and I was like I'm going out and this was the first time I was hanging out and my folks were like, yeah, apprehensive and nervous about who I was going out with and where, but we split anyway.

How old were you at the time?
I was thirteen. I think I was thirteen.

And you—
We bought three pints of Wild Irish Rose and we went to James'—this was one of the guys—we went to his house and his mother was out and we bought three pints of Wild Irish Rose and just drank it. And this was really the first time I used to drink. Because my mother used to drink liquor and she, but she . . . but it would be like a little bit of bourbon and all this water, she'd say, "This is for medicinal purposes." We always took it as a joke, yeah, ha, ha. My father never drank, he didn't drink anything, but some wine sometimes, and they had very few people that came over and socially drank. Most people came over to talk to my mother and console her when she got high, but I wasn't that experienced with drinking. But this time, I'm just drinking this wine and you know, just feeling good and kind of drinking and drinking, drank the whole pint. Well, I got on the train to come back to Brooklyn and I live in a project and there's . . . there are about five projects around me and I fell asleep and got off at the last stop. I got into the middle of one project and I was . . . I was just really drunk. I didn't know where I was . . . I knew I was alone. I somehow . . . I fell and my change went all over the street. I lay down in the middle of this playground and cried. I was like—man, I didn't know what was happening, so I went home. I remember getting home about three and my mother . . . it's really wild . . . my mom . . . my mom . . . she was really worried about me and she was up and when I got home she was in the bathroom and I had to throw up. She heard me coming and I knew I stumbled in there and I stumbled to my bed and I lay down and I just kept saying, "I hope she gets out

of the bathroom, I don't want to make a fool of myself."
And I threw up all over my bed, all over the floor. I got to
the waste can, didn't have nothing else to clean it up. I'm
thinking, I'm drunk but I'm clean. I said I can't let them
know I'm drunk. So I took my sheets off and changed
them. All of a sudden I got some sense and that's the first
time I started really hanging out and ever since then it
was like I remember my associations with these people
and realized for the most part I didn't want to be like
them. But, wait . . . I had a few more experiences before I
got myself together.

The next time I got really drunk in the morning. I think
this was a continuation of the same three people, the same
house. We were getting drunk off Bacardi. I went up . . .
I was really tiny, you know, I was really tiny. All my
friends were much older than me, they were much bigger than me and I wanted to hang out and I could put
away. . . . By this time this was like a little soap opera. By
this time I could drink. I could put away a pint of bourbon
and, you know, keep moving.

Can't do it anymore though?
Oh, no. So we were drinking. We went to Coney Island.
We played hookey, we were going to Coney Island. And
I . . . oh, man, yeah . . . I was with this fine fox, you know.
I was feeling good, this was like one of my little macho
manhood days. I had this little lady, you know, who was
drunk too. We were really tight that day and we were on
the roller coaster. We had dodged the police, we dodged
the truant officers, and all that stuff. We got there. We
were just riding around. They thought . . . there were so
many of us they thought we were a class trip. I got off this
Tornado, I'm drunk, boy, I'm laying on this sister and
somebody says, "Claude, there goes your mom, man."
And I go, "Like my mom?" Hey, man. I looked down and
I see this woman pointing at me.

What was your mom doing there?

Check this out, wait a minute. Check this out, there is even more . . . it was really fantastic. My mother had broken her ankle like two months before and she had been in bed. She had just gotten out now, but she loved Nathan's shrimp and like a friend of hers was . . . this wild, wacky friend had drove her down there to get Nathan's shrimp, so she was there and I saw the woman pointing at me and I saw my mother. I got straight, you know, real fast. I got in the car, you know, and my friends they were all in the car, they were saying like, "Wow, Mrs. James, let him stay, he's already here," and I straightened up. She said, "What are you doing here?" And I said, "I'm on a class trip," but I was drunk and she knew it. She knew I was lying. She said, "This is not a class trip." I got in the back of the car and my friends were all over the car saying, "Let him stay, Mrs. James." She said . . . she wasn't saying anything. Her friend, she was just checking me out, you know, giving me this look because I knew her. But she was blowing me away to my mom.

What did your mother's friend do?

Well, it's not . . . her friend is just going on, she's young. She's young. We're cool now 'cause we smoke herb together. Now at that time she's really into this, you know, "These young people, you can't trust them, you know," she said. "I thought Claude was a good kid and look at him out here," and I'm here . . . she's just going on. My mother is just sitting there and I said something like, "Shut up, fool," and I turned around and my mother looked at me and she said, "Just watch your mouth," but she didn't punish me and my father laughed when I got home because I was in shock. I can remember walking back to my building, I couldn't even walk, but I was walking like twenty feet ahead and it was like I was saying to myself, "You don't need no liquor." I was lucky, you know. I came here to get myself straight. I got help in time, you know. I mean, drinking isn't worth all those changes.

Tim, age 20:
How old were you when you started drinking?
At that time I was, let's see, I was . . . it must have been, I was fifteen; this was before I went to prep school: fourteen, fifteen. We had some wild experiences drinking in prep school.
Who was drinking like that in prep school?
In prep school? Hey, man, I was the bartender. I had like a business because, like I said, it was . . . it was fun to me. I could really relate back to being drunk or being really lit and having really fun times, so I would look for those times. I made this one batch of grasshoppers, which are like really strange green mint drinks that you make. I dug it, I dug the mint green, I was like, oh, a chemist for the group with alcohol, you know, and we would get lit and then that would last you through the week because you could laugh back on that experience. It was all deception, you know, because we weren't allowed to drink in our rooms.

They had all of these rules, but it was all this craziness that went on outside of the rooms. We had a makeshift bar, you know. I had the ingredients and I had a bar in our lounge and people coming over all the time, so it was really a moment for celebration and mischief.

Did you ever have any trouble in school?
You can't. You can't, they know it, they wanted to get rid of me because I . . . I've never been cool with any of my drinking or crazy stuff.

Could you get away with it there?
Yeah, more or less. You know, I mean, I got snagged on quite a few occasions. Luckily, Dorian was there because he used to rap my way out because I was very well liked.

Yeah, I was. You know, but I'd get over and I'd go off from there.

Well, recalling your experience, what advice would you give to other adolescents today in regard to drinking?
It's hard to say, it's really hard to say.

Why are you hesitating?
Because I'm thinking I could give them advice in relation to how I came through, but I think a lot of other kids today, they have a different head.

I think you're right, but in what way?
I think they're very . . . they're doing it much younger.

What do you mean?
There are some eight-year-olds who get lit up. I've seen them. Kids today are smarter than their parents.

Do you think teenagers can handle alcohol?
No, because adults can't handle it. They think it's a toy you know and the stuff can kill.

What made you stop?
One of my partners in school. We were tight all through prep school and when it came time to apply for colleges, we did it together. Well, we were freshmen in college and pledged for the fraternity. Man, they used to have some parties. We had this huge beer blast just before the Rose Bowl game. Well, Calvin really got fired up and took this girl up by the lake. Being drunk and everything, he got beside himself and started fooling around in the car with the girl. Well, he didn't have the emergency brake on and the car rolled into the lake. They almost drowned. I've never seen anyone so scared in my life.

How did this incident affect you?
Well, he just changed, you know. Like, he went from being eighteen years old to an adult real quick. I guess the fact that they could have drowned really frightened him

and that frightened me. I also thought about how much time I was wasting and the destruction. I mean, those fraternities destroy thousands of dollars worth of property and for what? Now, man, I'm finished for good.

Case Studies

Case Study One—Kathy, 19

Before I came to college I hadn't done much drinking and had never smoked. During the first week of school there were about a half dozen "get acquainted" parties which all served alcohol. There was beer on tap and plastic bags in garbage cans filled with vodka and orange juice. I had never seen so much alcohol in my life. Everyone had some drink in their hands and, so not to feel stupid and out of place, I got a beer.

I didn't like the taste of it very much but the screwdrivers were okay. I thought that since it was the first week of school all this alcohol was served to make people comfortable. Later I discovered that drinking was done, not only at weekend parties, but during school nights, and some people smoked in the middle of the day regularly.

Once as a birthday present for my roommate the people in my hall bought a keg of beer. That night I must have had about eight or more glasses of it. (When there is so much beer served at parties and things, you get used to the taste pretty quickly.) I know I shouldn't have had so much because I had a big chemistry test in a couple of days which I needed to do well on.

At first the beer didn't have much effect, or so I thought. We were all sitting out in the hall singing and carrying on but I was positive that I was not as wasted as they were. Then I decided to go study for my test. The moment I stood up my knees felt like lead and before I knew it I was on the floor again. After that my head started to pound incredibly and for the next three hours I was in the bathroom with those glasses of beer coming up one by one.

My roommate Mary finally had to put me to bed and I slept like a log until one the next afternoon. As a result I wasted a whole evening and morning, time which I could have had for studying. The chemistry test went so poorly that my professor said he almost didn't bother to grade it. Later that semester I dropped the course. I didn't realize it at the time but if I hadn't started drinking like I did I wouldn't have had to drop the course. Drinking had a direct effect on my school performance.

Case Study Two—John, 17

The people I hang out with have been drinking for a long time. Hell, drinking is nothing new. My parents drink all the time. My father used to come home from work drunk all the time, and he and my mother would have arguments about how he spent all his money on alcohol.

Around my block there isn't anything better to do except get high. School is boring so we hang around outside and listen to the radio, drinking or smoking. If a teacher walks by what can he say? "I'm going to call your parent" don't get nowhere these days. My mother doesn't care if I drink now and then, just as long as I ain't on drugs.

Mostly when we hang out, someone brings a bottle of wine or we chip in and get some Scotch and pass it around. Usually we would stay around school till it was late, then go home. I guess my mother knew I wasn't in school but she never said anything.

Some of the people in the group—Larry, Robert, and Dwayne—started doing burglaries. They would be around the school for a while then go out and break into a house and take stuff. Dwayne knew a guy in the neighborhood who would buy the stuff and then the three of them would split the profits.

Once I went out with them on a job. I'm not sure why —maybe just for thrills. Larry had been drinking a lot and I was afraid he was going to knock something over and we would get caught. When we got to the house there was no one in sight. The four of us climbed up the fire escape and forced a window open. Larry wasn't too steady and when he was going through the window his hand slipped and broke it. He didn't hurt himself badly but it made a lot of noise.

We had just moved a stereo, a couple of radios, and a TV over to the window when Larry just fell down, fainted out cold. I got kinda scared because we were going to get caught if we couldn't get him up. Then I heard sirens outside. One of the neighbors must have seen the broken window and called the cops. We still couldn't get Larry up so the rest of them were going to leave him there. I started to argue with them and they tried to drag me out the window. Just then, Larry woke up and we quickly got him onto the fire escape. We were lucky and the police didn't catch us.

Later I overheard my mother talking about blackouts. She said my father had had a couple of them and one time he fell down some stairs and hurt his back and afterwards couldn't even remember how he got hurt. She said the blackouts were caused by his drinking and that they were a sign of alcoholism. Then I realized that Larry had a blackout because he was an alcoholic and because of him I almost went to jail. From then on I stopped hanging out with those guys.

Case Study Three—Paco, 16

I started drinking when I was very young. I would drink at parties to have a good time; then I began to drink before school to get me through the day. If anyone had said I would be hanging out on a corner high a couple of years ago I would have laughed in their face. I saw lots of winos on the street near my house but I never thought that it could happen to me.

I dropped out of school in eleventh grade due to a difficult home situation. My mother got sick and there wasn't any money coming into the house. I found a couple of odd jobs that year like maintenance and being a security guard, but without a high school diploma a lot of employers weren't giving me a second look. I began to get frustrated after a while and to make life bearable I began to drink more. Even after I got my first job I kept on drinking just because I had gotten into the habit. That was probably the time when I became an alcoholic but I thought I could stop drinking any time I wanted to.

This went on for a couple of years. I would keep at a job for a short time and then quit, sometimes because they were boring but often because they were about to fire me for drinking anyway. Soon the jobs came fewer and further in between and I stopped looking for work. The street corners seemed to be the only place worth being, at least on the corner people cared about you and knew how truly rough it was out there. I spent more and more time on the corner during the day and at night stayed in a local bar.

One night around Christmas I was out on the street and was drunk. It must have been pretty cold that night but I couldn't much feel it and didn't much care. Down the street a gang of four kids was fooling around, knocking over garbage cans and drinking. They saw me coming and started whispering to each other. As I came further down the street they approached me, one holding out a knife. The one with the knife started waving it in my face and shouting things like, "You dirty drunk." Two of the other boys went behind me and knocked me to the sidewalk. I cut my lip and I just lay there, hoping they would go away.

They finally did go; however, I was too weak to get up. I must have been out there a couple of hours because when I could get up my hands and feet were frostbitten. I almost lost two fingers and a toe from that night and the doctors kept me in the hospital for a couple of weeks giving me detox treatments. I'm better now and staying off the streets but I'm still having trouble finding a job. I hope that I can stay off alcohol.

Case Study Four—Brian, 16

A lot of the kids in my school drink and smoke. Most of my friends' parents are psychologists and lawyers and we are used to seeing our parents come home and pour a cocktail or two. Sometimes I think if you took away my parents' Chivas, they wouldn't be able to treat anybody.

There really wasn't any particular reason I started drinking. I mean, my life was normal in that I had both of my parents and I had plenty of money. I guess I and many of my friends were just bored. At any rate we used to cut out of school and go over to each other's houses and get high. We generally would drink and smoke dope, but sometimes one of the kids would bring some other stuff that we would all try.

There generally was so much liquor in the bar that nothing was missed. Anyway, we would just get high and listen to music. We were actually very careful about how and when we did this, so we never were hassled by the school. Everything was quite harmless, actually, until Kimberly got blasted one day. I don't even know why we ever let her hang out. She was, you know, just someone who was always there—even if she wasn't invited. Well, we cut out of school one day, about six of us, and everyone came to my house. We were drinking whiskey sours, which I had learned how to make during one of my parents' parties. We were into one of our drinking games and we just began daring each other to do things.

At first, the dares were just simple things, like downing

a shot glass of whiskey or kissing someone. By four o'clock everyone was pretty well zapped so we began to clean up the apartment. Douglas had been teasing Kimberly all afternoon, without much response from her. Like I said before, she never really said much; I guess she just wanted to hang out. Anyway, all of a sudden Kimberly jumped off the couch and began screaming, "You're all a bunch of phonies." She was screaming hysterically and then she ran out to the balcony and jumped up on the railing. She kept yelling at us and daring us to follow her. Kimberly was always so quiet, we were really frightened that she was going to do something to hurt herself.

Nancy called one of the teachers at school and they came over. We finally got her to come down off of the rail. I don't think I will ever forget how Kimberly cried that day—it was really strange. I've never seen anyone cry like that. With the help of Roger, our physical education teacher, we gradually learned some valuable lessons. Kimberly had been a closet teenage alcoholic for years and we never knew it. The rest of us were well on our way. We have our own weekly groups to help other kids in the school. You know, if every kid who gets high off of alcohol could have heard Kimberly cry that day, I don't think any of them would ever drink again.

Case Study Five—John, 19

I guess you could say I was from a tough neighborhood. It wasn't particularly dangerous or anything to me, but everyone was kind of poor and people worked hard for what they had. My father had grown up in the same neighborhood and was always kind of tough on us. I guess he wanted to give us the things he never had.

Most of all, Dad was a dreamer. He had played some semi-pro baseball when he was younger and he always felt he could have made it to the top with a little luck and someone to push him. When he came home from working at the factory, which he hated, he would have some beers and tell us all about his ballplaying days. I guess, looking back at it now, that is how my problem started.

I had been playing ball for my high school team since my sophomore year. I wasn't that bad, but I wasn't that good either. I think I had gone out for the team in the first place to please my father and get him to notice me more. Well, he really did begin to notice me. Dad would pitch batting practice to me until I thought his arm would fall off and he would hit hundreds of balls to me for practice. At first it was kind of nice. I had never been particularly close to my father, because he worked all the time, and now I was getting a lot of attention. He pushed me hard and I have to admit I probably would not have been as good a ballplayer without his help.

The next year, things began to change. I had begun to think about going to college and when he found out about that, he nearly flipped. "The real money," he said "is made by men, not by any old college boy." He made me practice every day after school, after regular practice. On weekends he would work with me all day. I couldn't even date because I had to be in bed by eleven. You would think that all of this practice would have improved my game; well, it didn't. I began to get so nervous watching him in those stands that I just pressed and made mistake after mistake. The harder I tried, the worse I got. My coach kept telling me to relax, but it was impossible and my father was unmerciful. He questioned my courage and said I had "no guts." One day, after a particularly bad game, I cried and asked him to help me. He told me "Men don't cry," and said I was hopeless.

I think that was the beginning of a long slide for me that only recently has been halted. I don't know how I got hooked up with Tony and Ralph. I didn't hang out with them because I was considered to be a jock, which was really square for them. One day, though, on my way home after practice, Tony offered me a ride. Tony was a year ahead of me in school and was considered to be cool by many of the other students. Ralph was his partner and always seemed to be around him waiting and wanting to do his bidding. Maybe I was just tired or perhaps I remember so many times how my father would ironically say how drinking relaxed him. At any rate when I got in the car and was offered a "brew" I said, "Sure."

I must have downed it pretty fast, because Ralph in that dumb squeal of his hollered, "Look at my man tank-up!" Tony, in that cool way of his, never took his eye off of the road; he just said, "Hey, that's cool. Give him another." I don't remember how many I had, but I was pretty ripped when I got home. You can imagine my father's reaction. But you know, there was a part of me that didn't care how he felt. I remember laughing at some things also.

I began to drink fairly regularly after that. I guess I should have had one particular reason for drinking, but I really didn't. It got so bad, that I would regularly put away a six-pack and more after a year. The more I drank, the more I wanted to drink. Some of the guys on the team tried to talk to me, but as far as I was concerned I didn't have any problems to talk about.

Last October we had a big game against our arch rival. A win would have guaranteed a spot in the state finals. The night before the game, there was a pep rally sponsored by the school. Ralph and Tony and some of the other students were having a party after the rally to break night or watch the sun come up. Of course the players were supposed to leave early, but after telling my father that I was spending the night at a teamster's home, I doubled back.

I can't remember how much I drank that night. Maybe it was just a combination of the pressure of my father, school, and one year of sneaking around getting high with super seniors, but I got ripped. I remember waking up about two hours before game time and how dizzy I felt when the school band played the national anthem. This was the most important game of my high school career and I never got to finish it. It was as if everything caught up with me. I got sick all over my uniform on the bench and the next thing I knew I was crying and feeling that maybe my father was right, I didn't have any "guts."

I had let my teamsters down and even though they won the game, my inability to handle myself could have blown it for them. I was embarrassed, and others were embarrassed for me. About a week later, Vinnie, our first baseman, told me I had better get myself together. Vinnie is our captain and is six feet four inches and two hundred and fifteen pounds, so I listened. He told me about some rap sessions on teenage alcoholism that Father Dolan was conducting at the parish. I didn't think I was an alcoholic, but I didn't want to argue with Vinnie either; so I went.

It took about a year to get myself together. I'm in college now and during the summers I work as a peer counselor in Father Dolan's program helping other young people with their problems concerning drinking. My father and I get along okay now. I guess I've learned to say no to him when it's necessary and no to drinking when I'm having problems.

Case Study Six—Lourdes, 17

I drank because everyone in my family drank. I mean if you were born and raised in the barrio, there wasn't much else you could do. There are no jobs for our parents, so you know there are none for us. The schools are the pits, and everyone who lives here, lives to get high.

I watched my father give wine and beer to my little brother and he is only four years old. By the time I was twelve I could hold my liquor as well as most of the boys in my block. I never had any problem getting stuff. There are a million bodegas, bars, and liquor stores in the barrio, not to mention the private social clubs.

By the time I was fifteen I was downing almost a pint a day in the park during lunch or after school.

Sometimes I would go to my boyfriend's gang hangout and get high with some of the older girls. I'm not sure why I stopped, but I think my having gone to a parochial school helped. I began to see a couple of kids in school think about going to college. I remember how I always wanted to be a nurse and work at Metropolitan Hospital. Lisa was a volunteer there on Saturdays and one afternoon I decided to hang out with her. I helped her out in the emergency room for about four hours. I was really amazed to see so many people I knew in the neighborhood who were there because they got drunk and cut, shot, or beat up by somebody. It was really kind of sick. It was awhile before I got help, but seeing my people killing themselves helped turn me around.

Case Study Seven—John, 13

My friends were all older than me, either sixteen or seventeen. It just worked out that way. People my own age didn't interest me. They were so immature.

Most of the people who I knew drank, some regularly. I didn't really drink but since everyone else drank, I soon started to also. At first, I would make excuses as to why I didn't drink or sometimes pour a drink and hold it for a while. That way everyone would be on their fourth drink and I would still be on my first. Finally, Frank said to me, "You make me nervous when you don't drink." I soon got the message that if I wanted to hang around them I had to start drinking.

One of the guys got to use his father's old car because his family just bought a new one. It was pretty beat up, but at least it worked. On the weekend we would drive to a local beach and bring along a couple of bottles of wine. It was fun and I like being with people older than me who treated me equally.

One weekend I got busted. Not by the police but by some of my relatives. My friends and I had spent a couple of more dollars than usual and had bought a bottle of Scotch. I had had a couple of shot glasses and wasn't feeling too well, so I decided to go on the boardwalk and get some food. I was eating a hotdog when I really got sick and almost threw up. Just then some relatives of mine who were spending the day at the beach saw me and came over. My aunt didn't know that I had been drinking and just thought it was food poisoning or something. My uncle didn't say much at the time but as we were walking to a bathroom he told me that he could smell liquor on my breath, but he would let me off the hook this time. They drove me home and I went straight to bed. My parents never found out I had been drinking.

When I spoke to Frank the next day and told him what happened, all he could say was, "You just don't know how to hang out." He didn't seem to care that I got sick or even that my parents almost found out that I had been drinking. I didn't stay around that crowd very much longer.

11 Celebrities Speak Out on Alcohol

Jacob K. Javits, U.S. Senator from New York: "That anyone should be afflicted with a drinking problem is of great concern, but that any teenagers should be alcoholics is a tragedy.

"Our youth—our most precious resource—are the embodiment of our hopes for the future. They are the products of the richest and most diverse civilization the world has ever seen. Truly, their potential for exciting and rewarding lives is limited only by the imagination.

"Some experts state the cause of alcoholism among teenagers to be the enormous pressures exerted by our society to excel; others blame peer pressures. Whatever the cause, it falls to us—the adults—to demonstrate with compassion and understanding the world they lose as alcoholics that can be theirs if only each cared enough about him or herself."

*Joseph A. Califano, Jr., Former Secretary of the Depart-
ment of Health, Education and Welfare:* "It is time to
prove to the American people that alcoholism is not only
a treatable disease, but a beatable disease. . . .

"Alcohol abuse is a serious danger to teenagers. The
number of high school students who admit being intoxicated at least once a month nearly doubled between 1966
and 1975, from 10 to 19 percent.

"Alcohol-related accidents are the leading cause of
deaths in the 15-to-24-year age group; they account for
more than 8,000 deaths per year. In addition, more than
40,000 young people are hurt every year in drinking and
driving accidents—many of them crippled, paralyzed, or
otherwise disabled for life."

*William Scott, former principal dancer, balletmaster for
the Dance Theatre of Harlem; presently Director of the
Harbor Ensemble, and "Roots and Rhythms," Ltd. Company in Residence:* " 'Wine gives false courage; hard liquor leads to brawls; what fools men are to let it master
them, making them reel drunkenly down the street.' "
(Proverbs 20:1)

"How could anyone, let alone a teenager, drink something that has this effect? It's not a pretty picture."

*Bob Law, Program Director, WWRL, a popular radio sta-
tion in New York City:* "There is certainly teenage alcohol
abuse and I think that the reason for it has to be laid at the
feet of adults who have romanticized and glamorized alcohol use. Alcoholic beverage makers, in order to sell liquor, have presented drinking as a very hip, upscale,
glamorous thing to do, and even as a status symbol in
terms of maturity. Very often there are teenagers who will
pick up a glass even though they aren't drinking. It is
because they have accepted the notion that if you have a
glass in your hand you are mature. . . .

"One of the problems with alcohol is that it is presented as a legal, fashionable drug. When you consider all the very, very destructive drugs like heroin, cocaine, and angel dust which teenagers are willing to experiment with, to them alcohol becomes just a mild little toy—and teenagers are the victims of it."

Muhammad Ali, Heavyweight Champion of the World: "I don't drink or smoke. I never have, which is why I'm so pretty and still the champ. If you want to be the greatest, leave alcohol alone."

Charles B. Rangel, Congressman from New York: "Now that the drinking age has been lowered there has been an increase in the incidents of alcohol abuse by teenagers in the population. The cost of alcohol-related problems, such as vandalism, public disorder, discipline, and the like, is high in dollars and heartaches.

"Although I am concerned about the right of responsible young people to have a drink when they wish, I'm afraid that, as a result of the rise of alcohol-related car accidents among teenagers, legislators must re-evaluate the drinking-age question in order to see if there is some way that society is protected from the irresponsible youngsters among them."

Jim Cleamons, guard, New York Knickerbockers: "When the issue is alcoholic drinking, teenage drinking in particular, examine the facts before the decision is made to start. Alcoholic drinking is not a matter of age, but also a matter of responsibility. Responsibility to your health, both mental and physical, also a responsibility to your family, your friends and the community in which you live. This is not an issue to be taken lightly, so before you take that drink, obtain some facts and then decide for yourself. Question

—is this something you want, or is the indulgence because of peer pressure in order to be socially acceptable. Drinking is not for everyone, so before you start, get the truth of the matter. Then if you choose to drink, drink responsibly—be responsible for your future."

John Hammond, folk singer: "I can remember wanting to be 'hip' like a peer trying to be like the older guys. What should be remembered is that alcohol is a drug and abused more than any other drug. It can get to you in a bad way. Because it is legal, young people think it is not heavy, but it is probably the heaviest and as you get older it takes its toll. You don't have to find out for yourself to know it's bad."

Denny Greene of ShaNaNa: "In the last ten years, insufficient attention has been paid to the destructive effect of alcohol on Youth. Young people should be aware that alcohol is a dangerous and addictive drug which is generally abused. Why increase your problems and limit your opportunities by developing a crippling habit which will damage your health? Avoid alcohol as much as possible."

Philippe Petit, high-wire walker (World Trade Center, 1974): "Look, nobody is going to tell you what to do. If you are a teenager, and decide to lock yourself into drinking, great! Do it! . . .

You will lose your imagination; you will destroy all your energies; you will close, one after the other, all the doors to a wonderful world—the world of youth. Instead of being curious, determined . . . and alive, if you abuse alcohol, you will be surrounded by a gray wall, wherever you go; you will be "old," you will be "dead." There is nothing sadder than an "old child."

. . . . I am not saying never drink alcohol. After practicing on the high wire, what my body needs is a gallon of fresh-squeezed orange juice. A glass of cognac would be ridiculous. But wine, good wine, is not too bad a thing if you learn to know it, if you learn not to abuse it. . . . With a nice dinner, for a special occasion, to taste a glass or two of a very fine wine—nothing wrong with that. I appreciate good wines, but I'm not a drinker.

But, look, you are teenagers. You are old enough. Make your own choice! If you feel yourself living—like I do—that means you chose right. And if you meet someone leaning on the corner of his or her life, drinking alcohol endlessly—help them stop this crime against themselves."

Vaughn Harper, popular radio personality, WBLS: "Excessive drinking among adolescents starts out as proving your manhood to your peers. Then to some it advances to escapism in trying to lessen the pressures of everyday obstacles. So we're not just talking about abusing alcohol, but about abusing your Person."

Frankie Crocker, popular New York D J: "To be young is so beautiful. Alcohol provides nothing but ugliness."

12 How to Help a Friend in Trouble

BEFORE YOU CAN EVER BEGIN to offer assistance to someone you suspect of being an alcoholic, one thing must be made clear: The individual must want help. Otherwise, all of your good intentions, skills, and resources will go down the drain.

Actually, we are talking about two steps in the helping process. First of all, your friends must acknowledge that they have a problem. For a problem drinker, this is the most critical step he or she can take toward recovery.

I never saw myself as any alcoholic. Drinking to me was like smoking, you know? And I did both. They were just habits. I had some friends who tried talking to me but I just broke on them and fought. But when I was ready, you know, then I could deal with it. I mean I could see I had a problem. But saying it to myself and my priest, that was like the hardest part. . . .

Charles, 16

For a teenager, admitting an alcoholic problem to a peer is a very scary situation. Your friend at that moment is trusting you with information that potentially can make him or her very vulnerable in the world he or she lives in. We suggest that the first step you should take to help a friend in trouble is to *inform yourself.* In order for you to be able to be effective you must familiarize yourself with all the resources that are available. You might want to locate your local chapter of Alcoholics Anonymous. The AA chapters generally have open meetings at which alcoholics speak freely about themselves, their problems, their feelings, and their fears.

If you are not familiar with AA, check the listings in your telephone book for the closest chapter. Alcoholics Anonymous is still the most valuable resource available to someone who wants to know about alcoholics. Other resources you may want to explore are listed in Appendix VI.

The National Council on Alcoholism, Inc.
733 Third Avenue
New York, NY 10017

and

The National Clearinghouse for Alcoholic Information
P.O. Box 2345
Rockville, MD 20857

Many schools throughout the country have drug education specialists who can provide assistance to you. In New York City the SPARK program is an excellent example of an educational program that works with drug problems within the school system. Other resources may be health education instructors in your schools or your clergyman.

The second rule for helping is to use *your natural skills,* which are your ability to listen, your caring, and your willingness to help. These three skills, combined with the information you have obtained will help you to help your friend. Reinforce his or her determination to get help. Listen to, and even sympathize with, his or her pain; but be strong in support of your friend's need to get help.

The third rule is to respect your friend by *not preaching and lecturing.* Chances are that if he or she has come this far, the dangers and the effects of alcohol are clear. Your friend's illness doesn't mean that he or she isn't entitled to the kind of respect that all of us need and deserve.

Finally, helping does not mean forcing someone to agree with you. *Never threaten* a teenage alcoholic. In all probability your friend is defensive enough about the situation and, further, is living with a healthy amount of fear. Being supportive does not mean being pushy.

Your friend, like any of us who have had a long period of illness, may become tired and discouraged about being ill and begin to feel sorry for himself or herself. This is when he or she may be most vulnerable and most likely to start drinking again. Your strength, skills, and support at these difficult times can save something valuable—a future.

To sum up, in order to help a friend in trouble:

1. Know your resources.
2. Know yourself (your values, attitudes, skills, etc.).
3. Don't preach or lecture.
4. Don't threaten.
5. Help your friend to help himself or herself.
6. Help your friend get professional help.

13 Some Alternatives to Excessive Teenage Drinking

IN AN EARLIER CHAPTER we discussed some of the reasons why teenagers may drink. Certainly there are many powerful forces, including societal changes and economic changes in their nuclear families, which impact upon their lives and which may be significant causes for their drinking. (And let us not discount a phenomenon not uncommon to many teenagers who drink excessively: *boredom.*)

The concepts of alternative lifestyles to which we were introduced during the sixties have not been fully explored for the purpose of finding out their relationship to teenage drinking. Throughout the United States, particularly in large urban cities, there are increasingly mediocre performances in schools, fragmenting family situations, transient interpersonal relationships, and general disillusionment with society. Some teenagers, when confronted with these harsh realities, find drinking a quick, economical way of getting high and escaping whatever is troubling them. Counselors in the Boys Harbor Teenage Alcohol Abuse Prevention Program of New York City were often told by the young people that drinking helped them get through the day.

In the following pages we will discuss some possible alternatives for teenagers who drink too much.

Adolescence is a period almost consumed by energy and personal change. For many teenagers, the effective use of their energy and resources and management of their personal growth will allow for a rather smooth transition into adulthood. There are others, however, who are unaware of their resources. With time on their hands, nowhere to go, and nothing to do, they are prone to "get away from it all"; alcohol is one of many dysfunctional alternatives open to them.

Defining and understanding alternatives for adolescents is no easy task. In our work with teenagers we found it necessary to get them to understand their own resources, both internally and externally. Getting them to look at their internal resources requires a high level of risk, since it can involve a process of self-exploration that can be both new and frightening for the average adolescent. Discovering a new sense of self-worth and an inner strength which will allow the teenager to say no in a peer drinking situation may be frightening, as it may mean the estrangement of old relationships and a temporary sense of social isolation. It may, however, also mean the teenager is letting go (of old ties), which will allow for the development of new and more meaningful relationships.

To be able to take this type of risk, a teenager frequently needs an external support system to assist and encourage him. The work of Charles Seashore, a consultant in Washington, D.C., has greatly enhanced the success of our efforts in getting teenagers to define and understand their support systems. Seashore helps us look at these systems in terms of the kind of difficulty or problem a teenager may be facing at any given moment and the assistance needed. He identifies six different support systems and clearly shows us how we may satisfy their needs in a given situation.

CHARLES SEASHORE MODEL OF SUPPORT SYSTEMS

What the Teenager Feels	What He/She Needs	What He/She Wants
Social isolation	Someone to share concerns	Social integration
Vulnerability	Someone to depend on in crisis	Assistance
Emotional isolation	Close friend	Intimacy
Powerlessness	Someone to respect his/her competence	Self-worth
Stimulus isolation	Challenges	Perspective
Environmental isolation	Referral agent	Access to resources

The function of the model is to be able to move from left to right when one is in difficulty in any of these dimensions. If you are a teenager you may, for example, often experience a sense of powerlessness. If this is unidentified as a feeling, you may become increasingly frustrated or withdrawn. You may feel the need to be around other teenagers who also feel powerless and who drink excessively in order to feel competent.

If, however, you can identify those feelings of powerlessness, you may choose to responsibly meet your need by identifying those resources which will respect and stretch your competence and increase your feelings of self-worth. Identifying and utilizing your resources and potential support groups can be a constructive alternative to drinking. Let us briefly explore a few others.

Increasing Self-Awareness

Since the beginning of time, perhaps the most profound philosophical question has been, "Who am I?" Hopefully, this is a question that will forever lead you to new avenues of self-discovery, self-esteem, and personal power. Teenagers—in fact, anyone who perseveres in the pursuit of answers to the question—will probably avoid many of life's pitfalls which lead to excessive drinking.

The manner in which you attempt to receive your own self-awareness is varied. Here are some suggestions:

Personal Growth Group

Personal growth programs for teenagers have become increasingly popular. Many schools are now integrating a personal growth approach with their drug and alcohol education programs. Some of these programs, such as the previously mentioned SPARK program of the New York City Board of Education, are integral parts of the total school program. Other programs, such as Boys Harbor, Inc. or the Boys Club of America programs, work both in and out of school from a community base. Virtually all these programs attempt to get young people to improve their communications and decision-making skills as well as explore their values-clarification processes. Increasingly, schools and community agencies are utilizing some forms of group work to explore why teenagers are drinking. Check with the guidance counselor, the drug education specialist, or your favorite teacher about possibilities. You may also wish to contact the churches in your community; many have youth rap groups where the problem of teenage drinking is discussed. Most important, joining a growth group or some type of leadership program, such as the one sponsored by United Neighborhood Houses in New York City, can offer you the opportunity to make new friends while you learn something about yourself. It is to be hoped that you will feel more powerful, and the high you get from that is natural and productive.

Body Management

Taking care of one's physical self is rapidly gaining popularity in America. Jogging, swimming, tennis, or some other form of exercise is not only good for you physically, but when properly provided and consistently practiced gives a sense of accomplishment and positive well-being. You can develop your own personal program or join others. Alcohol, when used excessively, can be highly destructive to the body. If you or your teenage friends drink heavily, chances are you don't do much physically. Physical activity can be a healthy, fun deterrent to excessive drinking.

If for some reason you feel you are not athletically inclined, try some of these activities:

1. Tai-chi chuan.
2. Yoga.
3. Dance (fellas as well as girls).
4. Martial arts—Karate, judo, etc.

Nutrition

In keeping with a growing concern for what we do with our bodies is the increasing interest in nutrition. Although when used in moderation, alcohol can be pleasantly included in a diet, it is its excessive use by teenagers that is of such concern. There are, of course, rationalizations for almost any behavior, and you or some of your friends who profess to be health-food faddists and who abstain from red meats and pork may think nothing of consuming large quantities of wine and beer and heavy doses of marijuana.

An experiment suggested by Bob Fuller of the New

York City affiliate of the National Council on Alcoholism is indicative of how an otherwise good nutritional program can be offset by the overuse of alcohol. He suggests taking a shot of whiskey and, instead of swallowing it, hold it in your mouth against your inner cheek. You'll soon notice a burning sensation. This gives you a good idea of what whiskey does to the walls of your stomach, since the stomach walls are at least as sensitive as the inside of your mouth.

Be good to yourself; this includes watching and managing your food intake. A balanced diet will help you look and feel better.

The Other Side of the Mountain

In a lecture given at a National Training Laboratory session at Bethel, Maine, during the summer of 1977, John Bermon—philosopher, educator, and director of counseling at the Dooms Chaffee School in Windsor, Connecticut —talked about the ambiguity of life and how we are to live qualitatively. For all of us, the other side of the mountain poses threats or fears, or promises utopia. For teenagers these feelings or fantasies may be incredibly intense and at times terrifying. Those who have the necessary resources and support systems prosper. Others less fortunate resort to alcohol or other means to get them "over the hump." At Boys Harbor Mr. Bermon's concept of courage has allowed us to borrow from the Church, Zen, gestalt, and forms of meditation to help teenagers develop the personal power needed to battle the disease of alcoholism. Those of you—parents, teachers, and peers—who are helpers, and those of you who need to be helped should be aware of the untapped personal power that resides within each of us. When you can begin to utilize your own power, unaided by excessive drink or the use of drugs, that is the ultimate high.

14 How to Give a Responsible Party

THE INFAMOUS BEER BLAST, the all-night thumper contest, or the chugging contest, though exciting when they occur, can become a nightmare if you or one of your teenage friends become intoxicated and hurt yourself or someone else. You must try to give parties that are fun and yet conducted in a responsible manner, with social interaction and interpersonal satisfaction the main goals.

There are many ways to accomplish this. Here are a few:

1. Don't make booze the primary attraction of the party. There must be other attractions that make a party worthwhile. A party with drinking as its main theme does not have much meaning.

2. Make people feel at home without using liquor to break the ice. If your friends don't choose to drink, don't force them.

3. Encourage activity.

4. Always have non-alcoholic beverages on hand for your guests who choose not to drink—either because they have some responsibility to attend to or because they simply don't drink at all. Whatever their reasons, their right to them should be respected and soft drinks—in an amount equal to that of the alcoholic beverages—should be available to them.

5. Food is vital. It tends to slow the absorption of alcohol into the bloodstream and thus helps to avoid drunkenness. High-protein foods are especially good because they remain in the stomach longer. Cheese and crackers; Swedish meatballs; hardboiled, pickled, or deviled eggs; cheese fondue; ham sausage; biscuits; broiled chicken livers; cheese; pizza; and bite-size cold cuts are all high in protein. Crisp vegetables—carrots, celery, cauliflower, radishes, and the like—served with a protein dip such as cream cheese or sour cream are also excellent party foods.

There's no limit to the types of food that might be served. Load up on bananas, apples, grapes, pears, and oranges. Serve fruit salads, compotes, and ambrosias, with non-alcoholic piña coladas.

6. Non-alcoholic beverages should be just as exciting as alcoholic beverages. Bland non-alcoholic beverages turn people off and defeat the purpose.

7. Drinks should not be pushed on guests. If you are allowing your guests to serve themselves, there should be a shot glass handy to allow them to measure the alcohol they're putting into their drinks.

8. If you are serving an alcoholic punch, make sure it is made with a non-carbonated base. Alcohol is absorbed by the body much faster when combined with a carbonated mixer such as ginger ale. Fruit juice or tea is the best base for a party punch, but non-carbonated mixers such as plain water, juice, soda, etc., should be readily available at the bar.

9. The host of any good party must ensure that all guests are interacting with each other; if someone is drinking alone and excessively, an attempt should be made to get that person to join the others.

10. Stop serving alcohol an hour or so before a party is to end. By doing this, you allow guests to sober up. Coffee or some other non-alcoholic beverage can be served during the last hour. This will allow your guests extra time for their bodies to absorb the alcohol they have consumed, make it less likely that they will have a hangover the next day, and also have a safer drive home.

11. If one of your guests has drunk too much, ask someone to drive him or her home; if this can't be arranged, call a taxi or have him or her stay overnight. When guests have drunk excessively, the host or hostess has an obligation to prevent them from hurting themselves. It may even become necessary to hide the keys to a car or take other, more drastic action. Of course, one way to be an effective host is to control the amount of alcohol that is consumed at your party. It is better to have too little alcohol in your bar than to have too much.

If you follow the foregoing suggestions, your party will be not only responsible, but fun. With good food, good music, and a good crowd, the highs will come from the experience at hand and not be artificially induced by alcohol.

Party Recipes

Fruit Salad

2 baskets of strawberries	**raisins**
3 bananas	**nuts**
melons (in season)	**shredded coconut**
bunch of seedless grapes	**honey**

Rinse fruit carefully and cut bananas and melons into bite-size pieces. Combine with strawberries and grapes in a large bowl and top with sour cream. Sprinkle sour cream with raisins, nuts, shredded coconut, and add a little honey.

Serves 6.

Non-alcoholic Piña Coladas

1½ oz pineapple juice

1½ oz Coco Lopez creme of coconut

1 oz unsweetened pineapple

Pour ingredients into blender filled with ice. Blend until frothy, then serve.

15 Program for Reducing the Incidence of Teenage Alcohol Abuse

THERE IS NO MAGIC BULLET that will solve the problem of alcohol abuse among teenagers. But if you want to help limit the problem in your community or school, there are a number of programs that may be implemented. The criterion for the specific program you select should be your assessment of the needs of your community or school.

Don't be discouraged by individuals or "authorities" who will tell you, "There is no problem," or who suggest to you that your program cannot succeed. If your ideas are founded on a real need, if you have specific objectives, and if there is energy and support for the program, then in all likelihood the project will succeed. It is essential that you believe in your project and stick with it.

None of the models presented is foolproof. The effectiveness of each depends upon your energy, creativity, or perseverance.

Alcohol Information Dissemination

Alcohol education and information dissemination as a process to prevent alcohol abuse has come into disrepute as a result of the nation's experience with drug education and information. However, the failure of drug abuse information seems to have been less related to the use of the information than to the fact that the information itself was false, exaggerated, and often misleading. Once young people learned that marijuana was not automatically addicting, they became suspicious of a great deal of other so-called information and, as a consequence, ignored documented facts and proven dangers. It is therefore very important that the information about alcohol which is made available to young people be accurate and factual.

The mechanisms whereby alcohol education and information can be made available vary. Listed below are some suggestions:

Information Centers

An information center could be established within a community agency, school, college. It would be a repository of data concerning alcohol abuse, use, etc. A primary responsibility of such a center is to ensure that no stigma is attached to anyone utilizing its facilities.

Media

Making information about alcohol and its abuse available through the media can be done in a variety of ways. The school newspaper, community magazines, fliers, TV, radio, newsletters, etc. are all vehicles for disseminating information through the media. Even without personal contact, the media are important tools for making people aware of the problem of alcohol abuse as well as for getting them to think about how the problem affects them.

Advertisements

Using the disco market as a medium to promote alcoholic beverages, the liquor industry presently has a very active campaign directed at teenagers. One specific aim is to increase teenage consumption of wine. There was also an attempt by the liquor industry to make liquor available to younger children through the Kiddie Beer campaign of Anheuser Busch. However, in a test market in Virginia the community so vigorously protested the introduction of Kiddie Beer that the product was withdrawn from the market. To "fight fire with fire," advertisements can also be used to make young people aware of the problems of alcohol abuse and the potential impact of alcoholism.

Posters and Pamphlets

Creative posters and pamphlets can be very effective means of making a community aware of the problem of alcohol abuse. Pamphlets directed toward a community's or school's specific issue create more interest in reading the pamplet.

Open Houses and Displays

An open house or display concerning alcohol abuse can be an effective mechanism. Such a display might be appropriate within a school, a public building, etc. The project might provide demonstrations about the responsible uses of alcohol, the impact of alcohol on the body, quizzes to help young people analyze their personal drinking habits, displays of statistics concerning the cost of alcohol to the country, Breathalizer tests, etc.

Alcohol-Awareness Compaigns or Days

An alcohol-awareness day or a campaign to make the community aware of the problem of alcohol abuse might be established within the school or community agency or on a community-wide basis.

Panel Discussion

A panel discussion is an excellent way of encouraging dialogue about the problem of teenage drinking, and could be appropriate on any level. Participants could include teenagers, teachers, community leaders, clergymen, and other concerned people. The discussion, directed toward the problem as it confronts a specific community or a specific population, could take place over a number of days or be on a one-shot basis.

Film Festivals

A film festival might take the form of either government-produced or alcohol-abuse, agency-type films shown over a period of time. Another possibility would be to look at alcohol abuse as portrayed by the film industry. There are many movies portraying problems of alcohol abuse and alcoholics, and these could be shown to stimulate interest in the problem.

Speakers' Bureau

The establishment of such a bureau is needed in many communities, with speakers available to community groups, schools, clubs, civic groups, etc. to discuss the various aspects of alcohol abuse (pharmacology, legal, cultural comparisons, trends, pathology, etc.)

Breathalizer Campaign

Often, many people are unaware of how much they have drunk, and a Breathalizer campaign would be a means of making young people aware of the impact of their drinking. The University of Massachusetts has a drug education program conducted by Dr. David Kraft, which has operated a Breathalizer tester outside the university's campus tavern, where students can voluntarily measure their blood alcohol concentration and determine the extent to which they are intoxicated. This type of Breathalizer test gives young people immediate feedback on the effects of their drinking. A campaign to publicize the Breathalizer testers might be appropriate to a school, community, family party, community event, etc.

Peer Counseling

As previously mentioned, peer counseling can be extremely helpful in making young people aware of the problems of alcohol abuse; the resulting interaction also enables peers to influence the drinking behavior of their friends.

Small-Group Educational Programs

Rap sessions dealing with attitudes toward alcohol as well as other aspects of the alcohol-abuse issue might provide very appropriate and meaningful experiences for young people. The exchange and sharing of experiences can be enlightening.

Academic Courses

Within the school or college curriculum there might be courses offered on alcohol abuse. Alcohol has so wide an impact on society and has played such a very important role in the development of mankind, that a course on the subject would be very appropriate, either as a regular credit course or as a special mini-course. Such a course might focus on alcohol from a physiological, pharmacological, or pathological point of view. Another approach would be to look at alcohol from a historic or literary point of view. The landing of the Pilgrims at Plymouth Rock is credited to the fact that there was a lack of beer on the *Mayflower*. And just as the Anglican Church traces its origin to the seemingly irrelevant fact that Henry VIII had syphilis, resulting in stillborn offspring, so, too, are there innumerable other historic events traceable to the impact of alcohol.

Seminars

Seminars directed at professionals are an essential mechanism for increasing their awareness of the problems of alcoholism, about which many are rather naive. They have to assume more responsibility for such social ills and to exert leadership within their own professional groups and their communities. Seminars on a high-school level would also be appropriate for teachers, counselors, and even students, to discuss alcohol-related issues.

Individual Research

Since there are many aspects of drinking behavior for which there are no answers to date, an individual might wish to initiate a research project on his or her own to seek answers in the areas of, say, the impact of the environment on drinking; or the changing attitudes toward alcohol and how it affects alcohol consumption.

Role-Modeling

Each of us should examine our drinking behavior to see that we are setting proper examples for younger people

—for example, a high school student has a positive role to set for junior high school students. This does not mean that we must abstain from drinking in front of younger people, but rather that we should drink in moderation, show compassion for those who have drunk too much, and demonstrate the responsible use of alcohol at parties, as discussed in Chapter 14—that is, have non-alcoholic beverages on hand for non-drinkers, provide food to reduce the possibility of intoxication, and see that anyone who has overindulged gets home safely or is kept from leaving until he or she has sobered up.

Parental or Peer Intervention

While no one has the ability to totally prevent teenage children or friends from drinking, ways can be set up to encourage responsible drinking. For example, if several teenagers are going out and it is probable that they will drink, ask one of them to volunteer to abstain on that particular occasion so that he or she can drive the others home safely.

Transportation

In communities where the drinking age varies from one area to another, it might be a useful community project to provide transportation to young people who travel from a community where 21 is the legal drinking age to one where they can be served if they are 18.

Changing the Cultural Meaning of Drinking

All too often drinking is thought to solve problems, or one drinks to get drunk. There must be an attempt to modify these destructive habits and to encourage responsible drinking in situations which are recreational, so that the drinking does not become the primary focus of the activity.

Student Handbooks

The orientation handbook that young people receive when they enter a new institution should include a statement of the institution's policy on drinking and serve as a vehicle for dispensing information about alcohol. The handbook should also contain information about sources of help for those who abuse alcohol, provide suggestions for responsible drinking, and begin the sensitizing of the teenagers to their attitudes about drinking.

Student Government

All too often (at least when we were in school), student government was no more than an attempt to usurp control from adults (which is part of growing up); there was little attempt to develop positive programs within the student body. Student government has a positive role to play, if it is willing to accept responsibility for the behavior of its constituency. As a start, student leaders must look to their members for direction, not to the faculty. Once in tune with all factions of the student body, the student government must channel its activities in a positive, responsible direction and not appear to be the pawns of the faculty. For instance, a celebration for a school team victory can take the form of (a) a school-sponsored party with no liquor—which probably means there will be surreptitious drinking and a bigger bash afterward; or (b) a student-sponsored party with lots of booze, at which the majority of participants will get high and some drunk, endangering their safety and that of others.

But *there is an alternative*—the student government could plan an after-game bash which would follow the suggestions made in Chapter 14 and, in addition, highlight the accomplishment of the team, giving them the recognition of their peers.

Self-Policing Program

In many schools where drinking and illicit drug use are rampant, a program of self-policing might be instituted to prevent the abuses of a few from hurting the majority of the students. Participating in such a program would not mean being a fink, but rather providing education to fellow students and encouraging them to drink responsibly.

In Conclusion

ALCOHOL IS PROBABLY THE MOST MISUNDERSTOOD DRUG utilized by society. It can be a pleasurable lubricant for enhancing any number of accepted social situations. But it can also be destructive and addictive, leading to the ruin of one's life.

If you are an adolescent, you will probably be experimenting with alcohol as part of your initiation into "adulthood." We hope this book has taught you something about the dangers of excessive drinking and how, if you are going to drink at all, you can do so intelligently.

Remember that some of the important rules to follow in regard to drinking are:

1. Drink moderately.
2. Never drink to solve your problems.
3. Drink responsibly.

4. Don't drink to reduce stress.
5. Don't drink and drive.

Finally, we hope that all of you have the courage to say no when you have had one too many.

Appendix I: A Philosophical Framework for Preventing Alcohol Abuse

AS WE ATTEMPT TO DEVELOP PROGRAMS that seek to eliminate or reduce the extent of alcohol abuse among teenagers, it is essential that we do so within lofty philosophical constructs of man's potential. To have developed a program that only encourages a person to switch his drug of choice from alcohol to marijuana does not achieve anything. We have done something when we enable young people to feel better about themselves or to be able to effectively solve those problems which may have led to their drinking.

In approaching program development it is essential that we have a high regard for man and his relation to the Creation. We must view man as the highest form of creation, capable of unlimited development and potential, capable of perpetually moving beyond himself. We cannot place any limitations on our concept of man for if we do, we automatically diminish any results that might be obtained through efforts in his behalf.

All too often programs for teenagers fail because their developers and operators did not believe in what they were doing or had limited expectations of youth. Such an attitude, in turn, limits their own capacity and potential. It is the old story of the self-fulfilling prophecy. If you expect the students you are working with to fail, they will fail. Conversely, if you expect them to succeed, they will succeed. This concept has been scientifically proven by dividing a group of students randomly and telling one teacher that his students were superintelligent and another teacher that his were average. The result: the students described as superintelligent performed well; the students who had been said to be average performed averagely. It is therefore essential that we have high expectations and really believe in our goals—race, sex, regional animosity, etc. notwithstanding.

With a worldview of man as having unending potentialities, a good youth services program becomes the vehicle for translating potentiality into actuality at an optimum rate. Essentially, whether it is stated or not, what any good youth program does is to seek to enable young people to become self-actualizing or capable of achieving their maximum potential. In order to achieve their maximum potential they must become fully conscious of the learning process and take charge of it, thereby shaping their own destiny.

A person who is going to realize his potential is one whose learning patterns and habits facilitate unending growth and development.

How to learn is in itself something that is learned. Learning is not equally germane to the process of learning how to learn. The more that a person is able to learn, especially in the early years, the more competent he will be as a learner. Thus an ineffective learning habit precludes, inhibits, slows up, and places limitations upon the rate and scope of present and future learning. In short, a child can be taught a certain set of beliefs, attitudes, ways of thinking and behaving that will set him on a path of never-ending growth and development or he can be taught another set of beliefs, attitudes and ways of thinking and acting which will function to limit the rate and extent of the development of his potentialities. We learn how to be or not to be and therefore are able to become or not to become.*

In developing and operating a program to serve youth, especially one aimed at combating alcohol abuse, there must be a process through which we attempt to determine what is hindering a young person from developing his ** human potential and develop strategies to overcome that difficulty. Once the source of the suppression has been identified, efforts must be directed toward strengthening the problem-solving ability of the teenager and providing him with the necessary skills to overcome the suppressive factor. A young person can respond to his problems in any number of ways:

1. He can view the problem as a challenge, mobilize resources to deal with it, and thereby become stronger and more fully developed.

2. His behavior may become so stagnated or routinized that he just stalls and does nothing.

3. He may withdraw into a world of fantasies, drug abuse, alcohol abuse, etc.

4. He may react in an overly aggressive manner and act out the role of, or become, a troublemaker.

Problems and frustrations are an inevitable part of life, but it is the way in which these frustrations are handled that determines the growth or the structuring of the individual. An alcohol abuse-prevention and education program and simple guidance on a one-to-one basis must strive to encourage young people to develop positive feelings about themselves. To achieve the goal of a self-actualizing, fully developed person, the program must have three components:

---

* Daniel Jordan, "The ANISA Model—A New Educational System for Releasing Human Potential," *American Oxonian*

** AUTHOR'S NOTE: To avoid awkward sentence structures, we have used the masculine singular pronoun in most of this text. Everything written, however, is intended to pertain to female as well as male teenagers.

1. *A meaningful activity or task.* Involvement of a young person in a worthwhile activity is essential in that it enables him to feel that he "belongs," and develops in him a sense of usefulness and competence. The activity can be related to work, recreation, community-organizing, volunteer services, school—the possibilities are limitless. The important thing is that the young person see himself as contributing in a meaningful way to a task, process, or family.

2. *Acknowledgments of the young person's good points.* Making a young person feel good about himself and thereby helping him to develop a positive self-image involves, in a sense, an attempt at behavior modification (simple learning theory). This means that it is important to try to ignore negative behavior on the part of the young person and to take advantage of every opportunity to compliment and/or reward him for any changes he makes for the better or for any task he performs well. He will then begin to develop a positive sense of self and a realization that he has something worthwhile to offer society.

3. *Guidance in defining and solving problems.* There must be time in the program, activity, or family to help young people develop a framework wherein they learn how to solve problems and make decisions. Our approach at Boys Harbor has always been to ask young people to look at their problem and define all the possible causes for it, then to examine all the potential solutions and the possible consequences of each solution. This helps the young person to look at the dilemma in a rational manner. At this point it is incumbent upon the peer, parent, or youth leader to assure the young person that any decision he makes will receive their support. But no one working with young people should ever make a decision for them, because if it fails he will not only take the blame, but deprive the young person of the learning situation.

Appendix II: Planning Community Prevention Strategies

BELOW WE DISCUSS a number of possible approaches for preventing alcohol abuse that can be implemented by an individual or a group to have an impact on an individual, a school, or a community. This is not a definitive list of possible prevention strategies. You should not be dissuaded if someone says any of them won't work.

When embarking upon a project of any size it is essential to first make the following determinations:

1. What is the extent of the need? (Needs assessment)
2. What are existing resources? (Inventory of services)
3. Whom do you want to serve (and where)? (Target population)
4. What do you want to achieve? (Goals and objectives)
5. How will you achieve your goals? (Activities)
6. What will you need to get your project off the ground? (Implementation)

7. How will you know that you succeeded? (Evaluation)

The best chance of success is gained by:

—A precise needs assessment.

—Clear goals and objectives.

—Development of community resources.

—Good publicity.

—No competition or duplication of existing services.

—Good working relationship with existing agencies.

—No ego trips, but rather programs to meet real needs.

Needs Assessment

This process should be undertaken whether you are trying to assist a friend or work with a community.

It is essential in the development of any program that a careful needs assessment be made. All the parameters of the problem to be dealt with must be explored. In developing a strategy to combat the problem of alcohol abuse on a community or student level, some of the things we must know are:

1. What are the existing drinking patterns in the school or community?

2. What are the existing attitudes of the young people regarding drinking?

3. Where is the alcohol-abuse problem most prevalent?

4. Do the students and community see the drinking as a problem?

5. What is the impact of the alcohol abuse on the community?

A simple device might be a survey of the community to gather information. See Appendix V for a sample survey of alcohol abuse which was modified from the Boys Harbor Alcohol Survey instrument and the California Polytechnic State University Survey of Alcohol Abuse by Michael A. Looney.

A needs assessment for an individual might take the form of the following:

1. How much is he drinking?
2. Why is he drinking?
3. When does he drink?
4. What is the impact of his drinking on his behavior?
5. What is the impact on his family and are they admitting that there is a problem?
6. What are the treatment resources in the community to which to refer him?

Alcoholism is a disease and as such must be treated by professionals. Do not try to be a therapist.

If you are seeking to develop a program on a small scale with a limited number of young people, it may be that the needs assessment would consist of discussions with them to ascertain their needs and problems.

Establishing Goals and Objectives

Once the needs assessment has been completed and you have an understanding of the problem to be dealt with, goals and objectives should be set for the project, with the establishment of priorities among the objectives. Objectives should be measurable and quantifiable; this means that—

1. You will know when the project has succeeded.
2. You will have a clear idea of the behavior or attitudes you seek to change and know when the desired changes occur.
3. You have, given present resources, defined your objectives based on achievable goals.

4. You recognize you cannot save the world and be all things to all people, and you have defined the parameters of your ability.

The objectives must be very explicit and you must specify exactly what you expect the outcome to be. For example, the objective for a small project would be to identify 10 peers abusing alcohol and to involve them in activities that would inform the community of the problem of alcohol abuse.

Activities

Prevention strategies can be classified into two main types:

1. *Specific strategies.* These deal directly with alcohol and drinking, and attempt to reduce alcohol consumption. The strategies are quite varied and involve such things as alcohol education, modification of drinking patterns, and the influencing of the behavior of those who drink.

2. *Non-specific strategies.* These do not deal directly with alcohol or drinking. Basically they are strategies based on the belief that if a person is not bored, has something to do, is capable of making intelligent decisions, has friends, is competent and creative, then it is less likely that he or she will abuse alcohol. Non-specific strategies usually involve alternative activities to drinking.

Prevention strategies can also be divided into personal and environmental categories. Personal strategies make use of activities that involve people and affect their attitudes toward alcohol abuse (alcohol-awareness workshops, counseling, etc.). With environmental strategies, ways are sought to change the environment in which the young people function, establish responsible drinking policies, provide taxi service for intoxicated persons, etc.

Implementation

The general principles to keep in mind in the implementation of a program are:

1. There must be agreement on the overall goal and on the strategies chosen to achieve that goal.

2. Objectives must be specific so that they can be evaluated.

3. There must be leadership that has credibility with the young people as well as with the community.

4. The people that the project seeks to serve must be involved in the process. Adults or peers often feel that they know what's best for the young people and therefore they should make all decisions. However, the young people to be served by the program will make invaluable contributions to any program's development. Further, the involvement of young people enables them to feel useful, feel that they belong, and will encourage other young people to respond to the project.

The story of the good student helping the poor student comes to mind. In the good student's zeal to be helpful, he does the poor student's work for him. The poor student was struggling, but slowly getting the task done. As a result of the "help," the poor student never learned how to complete the task, and when he attempted the work on another occasion he failed because he had not learned the process.

5. It is important to look at resources in the school and community. Are there existing programs? Are there any facilities which your program can use? Who can provide you with manpower, office space, or funding? Who can help you?

Community development is essential to get and hold people's interest. If you are to have any success in curbing alcohol abuse you must shake people out of their lethargy.

It isn't an easy task, but it has to be done and done in a way that will stir positive action. It is important to increase the awareness of the community and to help various groups recognize what's needed and determine how to meet those needs.

6. It is essential to maintain high visibility to keep people informed of what you are doing or else you will lose whatever support you received initially. However, there is also something to be said for a low-profile campaign, working with small groups of young people. Many times people want to do their own thing with a group of young people and to have an impact in just a limited area. We think this is a positive strategy and one that should be encouraged. When striving to make a community-wide impact there is, as mentioned above, a need for high visibility, but there is also a lot of positive reward from small, individual, limited programs.

7. Any project that is established must have continuity with the young people and with the community. It cannot be haphazard. There must be consistency of activity. If it is perceived as being shaky, the project will flop.

8. Be creative. All too often projects die from lack of creativity, ingenuity, and energy. There is no foolproof formula for success, but we have found that any program which is energized and creative and involves young people will be successful no matter what mechanisms or activities are the focal point of the project.

It is essential that we not lose sight of the direction that the project must always have in focus; i.e., to enable young people to develop a sense of competency, usefulness, power, a positive sense of self, and appropriate ways of feeling about their environment.

Appendix III:
Ten Structured Experiences

SOMETIMES WE NEED ASSISTANCE in looking at issues or experiences that are important to us as we learn and grow. The ten structured exercises in this section will not prevent you from drinking or becoming alcoholic. They will, however, help you to look at those parts of you that you may not ordinarily explore. By using these experiences you may begin to identify new strengths in yourself which will help you to be responsible about your drinking. You may also discover weaknesses which may make you vulnerable in drinking situations.

These structured experiences are designed to help you:

1. Solve problems.
2. Explore your values.
3. Discover who you are in relation to alcohol.
4. Look at how you plan your life and make decisions.

Most of the experiences are designed for small groups. You might utilize these experiences in school, church, or in your living room with friends.

1. *Problem-Solving Guide**

A problem exists when there is a difference between what is desired and what is actual.

These steps to problem-solving are offered as a guide to help you solve problems efficiently.

Step 1

Define the Problem or Set a Goal

Clarify what the problem is; be as specific as you can. Decide who, what, when, and where the situation is problematic. Determine what the ideal situation would need.

Step 2

Diagnose

The problem should be tested to determine if it is a personal problem or a group problem. Information should be collected from as many sources as possible in order to get a complete picture of the situation.

Step 3

Produce Ideas

In this stage, try to come up with as many ideas as possible. One method of doing this is to "brainstorm." Share all the information and ideas you have. Put in the most "far-out" ideas you have. At this point, the number of ideas is important; the more the better.

Step 4

Evaluate Alternatives

This is the point to evaluate, clarify, summarize, and combine your ideas. Test for reality: with the resources you

*As developed by the N.T.L. Institute

have, is this idea possible? One effective method of doing this is to do a "force field" analysis.

Step 5
Decide on a Solution
From your list of alternatives, choose the ideas that most meet the goal or solve the problem and can stand up when tested in reality.

Step 6
Planning for Action
Now you are ready to assign and assume specific responsibilities. Each member should accept a specific task. The task should be stated and the who, what, when, and where should be recorded.

Step 7
Implementation
Carry out your specific task. Report back to the group coordinator or peer leader. Check with other members of your group. If you could not complete your task, check with other members to see how this affects them.

Step 8
Evaluation
When you feel the goal is met or the problem solved, go back to Step 1 to see if you have done what you set out to do. You can use some of the diagnostic methods from Step 2 to evaluate.

2. *Values Clarification*

GOAL: To learn to choose freely and responsibly.

TIME: 15–45 minutes depending on the choice of experience.

STAFF: 1 or more.

MATERIALS: Pencil, paper, newsprint.

PROCEDURE: The following is a list of open-ended topics to be used in small group discussions. Each statement is to be processed, looking for the consequences of adverse behavior (e.g., when I am alone, . . . I become afraid and get high drinking) and to give positive reinforcement concerning responsible behavior (e.g., when I am alone, . . . I have an opportunity to think about the work I have recently done well).

Small Group Discussion Outline

Most of all I value . . .

I feel that I belong when . . .

When I feel anxious or threatened, I usually (move against, move away, comply) . . .

To me, loneliness is . . .

Being a woman/man usually means . . .

I get most angry when . . .

When someone in authority blocks what I want, I usually . . .

When someone tells me a serious personal problem, I usually . . .

When someone gets angry with me, I usually . . .

Some people find it hard to give and easy to take; I usually . . .

Regardless of what others expect of me, I usually expect myself to . . .

My work satisfies my need for . . .

In spite of what others think, I am . . .

Variation: Ask participants, after alcohol workshop, to fill in statement:

When I drink . . .

3. *Build Me a Town*

GOALS: To examine our outlook toward the values in our society. To take a look at the necessities needed to build a new society. Consensus-building/decision-making within the group. Sharing values between group members.

GROUP SIZE: 15 or more participants.

TIME: 30–45 minutes.

MATERIALS: Large newsprint and colorful markers or crayons.

PHYSICAL SETTING: Large room.

PROCESS: Group leader initiates discussion about the values of our society concerning: (1) institutions and how they affect us; (2) police—the necessity of; (3) schools, etc.

Group leader tapes newsprint on the wall and hands out markers to all the participants. On the newsprint he/she may start the activity by drawing two lines resembling a road or a lake, etc. (not emphasizing what could be interpreted as a value).

Group leader then instructs participants to each, one at a time, go to newsprint and add something to the town he has started building.

Discussion and consensus of what to put is left up to participants. This will give them a chance to look at the structure of their society and what makes it up. Also to generate group discussion on personal values.

4. Self-portrait

GOAL: 1. To generate self-disclosure.
2. To explore self-image.
3. To see and hear how others view us.

SETTING: Large quiet room.

GROUP SIZE: The initial large group will be divided into sub-groups depending on staff availability.

TIME: 45 minutes.

STAFF: 2 or more.

MATERIALS: Large sheet of newsprint, colorful felt-tipped marking pens.

PROCEDURE: In large group facilitator.

1. Instruct participants to draw their own self-portraits on the newsprint, using markers. They are instructed that, in addition to pictures, they may use words, symbols, anything that could be descriptive of them in any manner they choose.

2. Participants then should go to separate parts of the room so that no one can see each other's portrait. No names.

3. When portraits are completed, have the participants fold their papers twice, not letting anyone see their picture.

4. The processing of the portraits should be done in two or more small groups. In the small groups the portraits should be placed in the middle of the floor and mixed up.

5. Each participant should pick one drawing out of the pile, not knowing whose portrait it is. He or she then should describe the person and decide who the person is using the data that is on the portrait. Others in the group can also give their opinions of what each portrait is revealing about the person. Finally, each individual will discuss his/her own drawing.

Question:	1. What does this picture reveal about the person?
	2. How does the person feel disclosing his/her private images within the group?
	3. How does the person feel about the feedback he/she has received from the group concerning his/her portrait?
Variations:	After discussing the first portrait, the group does a portrait of themselves drunk.
Evaluation:	What are three differences between the picture of you drunk and the picture of you sober? Or, after the first drawing and processing, another drawing can be made with the emphasis on (1) how participants may see themselves ten years from now, or (2) how each participant may like to be.

5. Insights

GOAL:	To enable students to gain insight about their behavior and others' behavior as it is affected by alcohol.
TIME:	Approximately 45 minutes.
STAFF:	1.
MATERIALS:	Pencils, paper, newsprint, forms.

PROCEDURE: Have the students complete the following categories with at least five ideas. The ideas should be their own and not society's.

Because I am an Alcoholic I Must	Because My Friend is an Alcoholic I Should	Because You are an Adult Alcoholic I Must	If My Teacher Were an Alcoholic I Would

Questions: What did you learn from doing this exercise?

Did you find it difficult to differentiate between your own ideas and society's ideas?

Is everyone's identity shaped by outside forces. If so, how?

What were the reasons for writing what you did for each category? (What experiences were your expectations based upon?)

Theory: An assumption may be made that individuals who feel good about themselves and others are healthy. Adolescents who have difficulty understanding who they are as individuals may potentially create rigid expectations or fantasies concerning others. These conflicts may result in frustration leading to alcohol abuse.

6. Autobiographical Questionnaire

GOAL: To enable students to get to know each other by comparing similarities in their lives.

TIME: 45 minutes.

STAFF: 1 or more.

MATERIALS: None.

PROCEDURE: The group is to break up into dyads (groups of two) and go off into a quiet section of the room. They are to ask each other questions in order to complete the statement, "I am the same as you because. . . ." They are to complete this statement as many times as they can in 10 minutes. After 10 minutes, the dyads are asked to join another dyad and continue with the same process for another 10 minutes. They will then join together with another quadrad and complete the preceding process. After the task has been completed, they discuss what they learned about each other.

Variation: Group leader instructs participants to form dyads and discuss: (1) "I am the same as you because I need alcohol to have a good time at a party." (2) "I am the same as you because I can't socialize with the opposite sex unless I have a drink." (3) "I am the same as you because my parents drink too." Participants then come back in the circle and have open discussions on the above topics.

7. Simulation and Role-Playing: "Who Am I"

GOAL: To simulate situations concerning behavior during varying periods of alcohol intake, via role-playing.

TIME: Approximately 30 minutes.

STAFF: 1.

MATERIALS: Paper and pens.

PROCEDURE: Ask the students to complete the following sentences in simulated behavior at a party.

1. Before my first drink I am feeling . . .
2. After my first drink I am feeling . . .
3. After my second drink I am feeling . . .
4. After my third drink or more I am feeling . . .
5. The next morning, when I wake up, I am feeling . . .

Questions: Do you think that a person's personality changes after several drinks?

What personality change do you go through after you've had a couple of drinks?

How did you feel while you were drunk compared to when you were sober?

Has your perception of your drinking limit changed?

Theory: The purpose of this exercise is to allow people to simulate their fantasies and/or realities concerning behavior encountered while drinking. Students may be able to look at, through the fish-bowl experience, different simulated behavior during varying periods of alcohol consumption.

8. Reflections

PHYSICAL SETTING: Large room.

TIME: 30 minutes to 1 hour.

GOALS: To have the group look at issues surrounding alcoholism in and around their communities and to talk about different preventive measures that can be taken to curtail this disease.

MATERIALS: None.

PROCEDURE: The group leader begins the discussion by asking the group members if they've ever encountered an alcoholic on the street or perhaps on Skid Row and, if so, what were their feelings toward the alcoholic and how did they react to him or her. From that point, the group leader can ask the group to take a critical, analytical view about the growing alcoholic problem that is prevalent in our society today and what preventive measures might be taken in the fight to eliminate it.

9. Decisions

GOAL: To look at issues created around making decisions. To facilitate the process of solving problems.

TIME: 45 minutes.

STAFF: 1.

MATERIALS: Paper, pencils, newsprint.

PROCEDURE: Write a letter to yourself about your life or about taking care of yourself, or about a choice you are facing in the near future. Fantasize a discussion with yourself about a decision you need to make. Begin to discuss the decision with yourself. For example, whether to go back to school, to go to graduate school, to accept a new job opportunity, or whether to have a baby. Imagine you have a board of directors that is helping to make this decision. Who are the members of the board? Who is the treasurer of the board? Who has the most votes on the board?

Variation: Write a letter to yourself about your projected plans for your life in the future. Think about planning a future for you and your family (consisting of your spouse and children) and ask yourself how you will reach these goals.

10. Problem-solving (Freedom and Responsibility)

GOAL: To learn to choose freely between conflicting issues of freedom and responsibility in an attempt to build skills necessary in the solving of problems.

TIME: 15 minutes.

STAFF: 1.

MATERIALS: None.

PROCEDURE: Select a decision you need to make about your career. Choose two people in the room whom you know to feel differently about the degree of freedom and the responsibility individuals should exercise with respect to their lives.

Sit between these two people; freedom on one side, responsibility on the other. Have a discussion about your decision with each of them arguing with you and each other about the direction you should take. The rest of the group may eventually join in according to their preference. Ultimately the members of the group may want to vote by positioning themselves in terms of their own preference as to the importance of freedom and responsibility.

Questions: (to participant with problem)

1. Did the exercise have any effect on your decision? If so, what statements led you to that decision?

2. Were any new dimensions to your situation brought forth?

3. Did you feel comfortable playing your roles? Would they have been your natural choices?

(to group: general reactions/observations of the process)

1. Could you identify with the problem?

2. Which side would you take?

Appendix IV: The Harbor Teenage Alcohol Abuse Prevention Program: A Prototype Model

A Program Model

Boys Harbor Teenage Alcohol Abuse Prevention Program, sponsored by Boys Harbor, Inc., 1 East 104 Street, New York, N.Y. 10029, is a peer counseling model which seeks to reduce the incidence of alcohol abuse among teenagers by making them aware of information about alcohol and alcohol abuse as well as enabling them to develop emotional competence for values clarification, decision-making, and communication skills development.

The concept of the peer counseling approach was developed from the Harbor's experience with South Bronx gangs in 1972 and 1973. The Harbor developed a program that sought to assist gangs to develop positive programs for their neighborhoods. The thrust of the program was to reduce gang-related violence through gang sponsorship

126

of community improvement projects. What struck us most about the gangs was their positive peer interaction. One always assumes that all aspects of gangs are negative. However, the peer process of the gangs was a strength that the law enforcement officials in other programs overlooked as an option for rechanneling gang energy into positive endeavors; instead, the approach adopted was to kill off gangs through harassment, arrests, etc. The peer process operating within gangs was a means of survival in that the gang members took responsibility for each other. Gang members boasted and could prove that they were able to detoxify junkies, and they helped many young people who were on drugs to become self-sufficient individuals. The gangs also had strict behavior codes that were adhered to unswervingly. There was always a sense of community and camaraderie among the gangs and a very cohesive atmosphere.

In developing the Teenage Alcohol Abuse Prevention Program we sought to capitalize on the normal peer interactions and peer pressures existing among adolescents. We saw the peer process as being a means of making alcohol education more acceptable to teenagers as well as having peers intervene and improve the drinking behavior of other teenagers. In our goals and objectives, the Teenage Alcohol Abuse Prevention Program was based upon the assumption that if young people knew more about themselves, were better able to solve problems, and knew about the effects of alcohol, they would become more responsible drinkers.

Therefore the program's first goal is to reduce the incidence of adolescent alcohol abuse and to enable young people to be more responsible drinkers. The second goal is to provide adolescents with insight into their personal problems and help them develop the necessary skills that will enable them to deal with these problems without using alcohol.

Project Model

Essentially the program involves the following five steps:

1. Contracting with schools and teachers to allow us to operate the program.
2. Orientation of teachers.
3. Selecting peer counselors from within their classes.
4. Training peer counselors to conduct alcohol awareness workshops.
5. Peer counselors conduct 5 to 10 alcohol awareness workshops within the classroom.

Entry into the School System

The process of entering a school system as a community agency can be a complicated and political process which will undoubtedly frustrate most individuals; but it is important to be persistent, have credibility, and present the school with a responsible program. The manner in which one gains entry into a school system will vary from system to system. Within New York City. the usual process is (a) to contact the community school board, if it is on a junior high school level; or contact the Central Board of Education, if it is a high school; (b) To visit the principal; and (c) depending on the structure of the school, the principal will either direct you to the parents' association or a parents' advisory committee to get their approval or put you in contact with the specific teachers with whom you would be working.

Teacher Orientation

An orientation meeting is held with the teachers who will be involved in the program to make them aware of the process and to get their support for the program. The support of teachers is essential when the peer counselors come into the classroom to conduct the workshops. A teacher's positive attitude toward the project will greatly facilitate its success.

Peer Counselor Selection

The procedure for selecting peer counselors is as follows:

1. The trainer or counselor asks the students to define leadership, possibly using modern-day examples of leaders such as Martin Luther King, Jane Fonda, Jimmy Carter, General Patton, or Julius Erving. The students are then asked to identify the leadership qualities in each of these individuals.

2. The trainer initiates a brainstorming session to identify the qualities of a positive peer leader.

3. The class undergoes a self-assessment to determine their own leadership resources and to determine what they as a group would be looking for in a peer leader to conduct the workshops.

4. The class will determine by which procedure they want to select the peer counselor.

Boys Harbor determined that it is important that a win/lose factor not be established in the selection process. Therefore we usually took the two or three students whom the class generally felt were leaders. Special care was taken to ensure that those students selected were receiving skills that would be *shared* with others upon the completion of the program.

Training of Peer Counselors

The Harbor train peer counselors within the school, at our facilities in Manhattan, and at our camp facility in

East Hampton, Long Island. The average training session lasts 45 minutes, or one school period, and takes place two to three times per week. Trainees also undergo an intensive training weekend at our camp; we found them most receptive and enthusiastic about participating. Here is a synopsis of the training cycle:

Session1. Introduction to group process and explanation of the program.

Session 2. Pre-test (the program had an extensive research component and this second session was used to test the peer counselors for the evaluation).

Sessions 3, 4, 5. Modes and methods of learning—open-theory system and how groups function effectively.

Sessions 6, 7, 8. Values clarification. To learn to choose freely, issues of freedom and responsibility.

Session 9. Interventions, strategies—timing, appropriateness, need.

Session 10. Methods of feedback.

Session 11, 12. Physiology of alcohol—how it affects the human system, the diseases it can cause.

Session 13. Short-term counseling—crisis intervention.

Session 14. Personal style—effectiveness of trainees' delivery.

Session 15. Alcoholism—theory of causes, family effects, etc.

Session 16. Community resources to assist persons with problems of alcohol abuse.

Peer Counselor Implementation

Upon completion of the training program, each peer counselor conducted five to ten alcohol awareness workshops under the supervision of the trainer. The peer counselors essentially designed their sessions around alcohol education and basic group processes. Upon completion of each session the peer counselor's work was processed by the trainer, whose role in the classroom at this time is that of a process observer.

Questions concerning the Teenage Alcohol Abuse Program of Boys Harbor may be directed to:

Dr. Robert North, Project Director
or
Mr. Richard Orange, Jr., Training Director
c/o The Harbor for Young Men and Women
1 East 104th Street
New York, NY 10029

Appendix V: The Harbor Teenage Alcohol Abuse Survey*

CODE NAME

Directions: To create your TAAPP CODE NAME, please read each rule carefully and print the correct letter for each on the left-hand line.

PLEASE PRINT CLEARLY AND IN CAPITAL LETTERS

_____ First letter of your middle name (if no middle name, write X)

_____ First letter of month you were born in

_____ First letter of your sex: Male or Female

_____ First letter of the name or number of your street

_____ First letter of your mother's first name (if unknown, write X)

* Modified by Michael A. Looney from the Boys Harbor Alcohol Survey (copyright © 1978 by Boys Harbor, New York City, N.Y.) and the California Polytechnic State University Survey of Alcohol Abuse.

INFORMED CONSENT

This questionnaire has been constructed in accordance with the recommendations of the U.S. Department of Health, Education and Welfare in protecting against undue invasion of privacy. Participation is voluntary and all responses will be kept strictly confidential and used only for program evaluation purposes. You have the right not to answer this questionnaire or participate in the evaluation of the Boys Harbor Teenage Alcohol Abuse Prevention Program.

DIRECTIONS

This questionnaire is divided into two (2) sections. Each section begins with a direction page which explains how you are to respond to the questions in that section. Read the direction page for each section carefully and follow along with the administrator before beginning to answer the questions.

Age_____ Grade_____

PART A

We would like you to begin by answering a few questions about your drinking behavior. If you don't drink, you can tell us that, too. Please listen carefully to the directions and mark your questionnaire as honestly as you can. We will be using the term, "a drink," in several of the questions to come. Let's define that term. *A drink* means—

one can of beer (12 oz)

or

one glass of wine (4 oz)

or

one shot of hard liquor (1 oz)
(gin, vodka, Scotch, rum, etc.)

Now please think about when you drink, where you are, and who you're with. If you don't drink, mark that answer now and please listen until we come to questions that don't deal directly with drinking.

I don't drink _____

1. When you have a drink (look at the drawing on the previous page), you are usually

    alone _____ with friends about your age _____
    with your parents _____ with other adults _____
    with somebody else not named above _____

2. Where do you usually have a drink? (check all the places that fit)

    at home _____ at a friend's home _____
    at parties _____ around the block after school _____
    some other place (tell where) _____

3. When do you usually have a drink?

    at school, at lunch time _____ at school, other times _____ at work, lunch _____ at work, other times _____ some other times (tell when) _____

4. If you are drinking for about an hour, how many drinks would you take? (remember how we defined a drink)

    1 _____ 2 _____ 3 _____ 4 or more _____

5. On what days of the week do you usually have a drink?

    Circle each day on which you are likely to have a drink.

    Sun   Mon   Tues   Wed   Thurs   Fri   Sat

    Now put a big X on the day when you regularly have a drink, if there is one for you.

6. When you drink, what time of day is it usually? (Check all that apply)

Before breakfast ____ with breakfast ____
Between breakfast and lunch ____ with lunch
____
Between lunch and dinner ____ with dinner ____
Between dinner and bedtime ____ in bed ____

Now put a big X next to the line showing the time of day that is "regular" for you if there is one.

7. How old were you when you began to drink "on your own"?

    Years _____ Months _____

8. Now try to recall the last 30 days, and check the number of times you had a drink, got high, or got drunk. Let's define those last two words.

    High: A pleasurably noticeable effect without going beyond socially acceptable behavior, e.g., "feeling good," slight fuzziness about what is going on, or drowsiness.

    Drunk: Marked loss of control over ordinary physical activities such as staggering, confused speech, not knowing what is going on, nausea, or passing out.

	Never	Once	2–3	6–7	8–9	10 or more
Had a drink						
Got high						
Got drunk						

People give a lot of reasons for drinking. Here are what some young people have given as their reasons:

How often do you use each of the reasons?

If you don't drink, mark here ____ and then please answer the way you hear your friends talk about their drinking.

	Most of the time	Some of the time	Never use

9. I say I drink because:

   I'm old enough   _____   _____   _____
   It makes me happy   _____   _____   _____
   It relaxes me   _____   _____   _____
   I like the taste   _____   _____   _____
   My friends drink   _____   _____   _____
   It gives me courage   _____   _____   _____
   It makes it easier
     to talk to the
     opposite sex   _____   _____   _____

10. I say I drink to:

   Celebrate   _____   _____   _____
   Forget my problems   _____   _____   _____
   Get high   _____   _____   _____
   Feel sociable   _____   _____   _____
   Get "in the groove"   _____   _____   _____
   Show I'm grown up   _____   _____   _____
   Work better   _____   _____   _____
   "Rap" better   _____   _____   _____
   Have fun   _____   _____   _____
   Be one of the group   _____   _____   _____
   Be friendlier   _____   _____   _____
   Feel better   _____   _____   _____

11. How many of your friends drink?
    None ___ One ___ Several ___ Most ___ All ___

    I don't know whether my friends drink ___

12. Has your drinking ever hurt or broken a relationship
    with a friend? Don't drink ___ Don't know ___
    No ___ Yes ___

13. Has a friend's drinking ever hurt or broken his/her
    relationship with you? No ___ Yes ___ (Tell about
    it if you want to)

14. Has your drinking ever resulted in another person
    getting physically hurt? Don't drink ___ Don't know
    ___ No ___ Yes ___

15. Has your drinking ever resulted in damage to property? Don't drink ____ Don't know ____ No ____ Yes ____

16. Do you drink in front of your parents?
Don't drink ____ No ____ Yes ____

17. When you drink, do you feel guilty?
Don't drink ____ Feel very guilty ____ Some ____
None ____

18. How many times have you used marijuana in the past 30 days? (For example, sharing a joint twice a week for 4 weeks is 8 times)
Never used ____ Once ____ 2–3 times ____ 4–5 times ____ 6–7 times ____ 8–9 times ____ 10 or more times ____

19. How many times in the past 30 days have you used marijuana and had a drink at the same time?
Never ____ Once ____ 2–3 times ____ 4–5 times ____ 6–7 times ____ 8–9 times ____ 10 or more times ____

PART B

Directions

Please answer the following questions, whether you drink or not. Each is a statement with which you can agree or disagree. If you Strongly Agree, circle the SA under the statement. If you Agree, circle A. If you Disagree, circle the D. If you Strongly Disagree, circle SD. *Only* if you really can't make up your mind, circle U for undecided.

1. Alcohol is a dangerous drug.

    SA A D SD U

2. Drinking alone is no worse than drinking with others.

    SA A D SD U

3. People who drink are dependable.

   SA   A   D   SD   U

4. At a party, if you are not drinking, you would hide that fact.

   SA   A   D   SD   U

5. Drinking a pint of alcohol quickly can kill a person.

   SA   A   D   SD   U

6. The effect that alcohol has on a person depends on body weight.

   SA   A   D   SD   U

7. Eating slows the rate that alcohol gets into the blood.

   SA   A   D   SD   U

8. The liver can safely break down one ounce of alcohol per hour.

   SA   A   D   SD   U

9. Blacking out is an early sign of alcoholism.

   SA   A   D   SD   U

10. There is nothing wrong with taking a drink or two to relax.

    SA   A   D   SD   U

11. Getting high on alcohol at a party is harmless fun.

    SA   A   D   SD   U

12. Alcohol can be used responsibly.

    SA   A   D   SD   U

13. Drinking alcohol does not affect one's physical health.

    SA   A   D   SD   U

14. Drinking alcohol does not affect one's emotional health.

    SA   A   D   SD   U

15. Young persons should be allowed to decide for themselves whether they should drink or not.

    SA   A   D   SD   U

16. Alcohol requires no digestion. It passes directly into the bloodstream and is carried to all parts of the body.

    SA   A   D   SD   U

17. Alcohol is described medically as a depressant (downer).

    SA   A   D   SD   U

18. There are several kinds of alcohol, but ethyl alcohol is the one contained in alcoholic beverages.

19. After having several drinks you cannot operate a machine as well.

    SA   A   D   SD   U

20. A respectable family background, good education and success in business will keep a drinker from becoming an alcoholic.

    SA   A   D   SD   U

21. All things being equal, when two people of different body size (e.g., 130 lbs and 250 lbs) drink equal amounts of alcohol, the effect will be the same for each.

    SA   A   D   SD   U

22. An alcoholic is a person who can't leave alcohol alone even for a day.

    SA   A   D   SD   U

23. A good whiskey contains some of the vitamins and minerals necessary in the daily diet.

    SA   A   D   SD   U

24. Food in the stomach slows down how fast you get drunk.

    SA   A   D   SD   U

Appendix VI: Programs, Resources, and Literature on Alcoholism

IT HAS BEEN SAID MANY TIMES that there is nothing new under the sun, and the same may be said of program ideas for the prevention and treatment of alcohol abuse. If you are going to initiate a program for these purposes, there is probably no idea that has not been tried already. It always seems ludicrous that the government funds programs which they call innovative. What it comes down to is who can give a lot of "pizazz" to an old idea. We think that what the government should be funding are programs that work; then they should work toward dissemination of these models.

In this vein we would like to cite the National Institute on Alcohol Abuse and Alcoholism, which has done just that. Rather than continually waste money or try to find new ideas—which, to repeat, are only old ideas rehashed —they have spent money to facilitate the replication of program models that have proved successful in various communities. A model may be successful in one community, but not in another, and one of the goals of the replication project of NIAAA is to determine the variables which will allow a specific program model to be successful. Their question is, "In what types of communities will this specific model be effective?"

To obtain information on their program development, there are two divisions of the NIAAA to contact: the Prevention Division and the Treatment Division. It should be noted that the Treatment Division has also sought to develop program models to test their effectiveness. Whether or not they eventually replicate these models remains to be seen.

It is difficult to ever give the name of a person to contact in a particular division in the government as there is great movement in jobs and transfers and reorganizations. Therefore we list below only the division names and addresses. On the national level, there is:

The National Institute on Alcoholism and Alcohol Abuse
5600 Fishers Lane
Rockville, Maryland 20852

The Prevention Division
The National Institute on Alcohol Abuse and Alcoholism
5600 Fishers Lane
Rockville, Maryland 20852

The Treatment Division
The National Institute on Alcohol Abuse and Alcoholism
5600 Fishers Lane
Rockville, Maryland 20852

The NIAAA also funds two agencies over which they have very tight control and which they directly oversee: The National Clearing House for Alcohol Information and the National Center for Alcohol Education. The first is a repository of information on all aspects of alcohol, ranging from treatment of its abuse to distilleries. The second is charged with the responsibility of developing educational materials for the prevention of and education in alcoholism and alcohol abuse. Their addresses are as follows:

> The National Clearinghouse for Alcohol Information
> Box 2345
> Rockville, Maryland 20852

> National Center for Alcohol Education
> 1601 North 10th Street
> Arlington, Virginia 22209

All the divisions of the NIAAA are extremely cooperative and willing to extend themselves to be of assistance. Boys Harbor has had a working relationship with them over the past five years and we have never found them to be anything but productive and positive.

In approaching the NIAAA, however, you should have a general idea of what you want to do. To go to them on a "fishing expedition" would be a waste of your time and theirs. It is best to have first conducted a needs assessment, either in the educational or program development areas, so that you can be as precise as possible about what you want them to give you.

Another outstanding resource in many areas is the National Council on Alcoholism. This organization conducts research into alcoholism and alcohol abuse, lobbies for legislation for their treatment, and generally has made an exceptional effort to make the public aware of both the dangers of alcohol abuse and the treatability of alcoholism. Their address is:

> The National Council on Alcoholism
> Two Park Avenue
> New York, New York 10016

The National Council will be able to provide you with literature of all kinds, technical assistance, names of available lecturers on the subject in your area, as well as information on the latest research.

And, of course, there is Alcoholics Anonymous, which is the most successful of the agencies responding to the problem of alcoholism. Check your telephone directory for the chapter nearest you.